P9-CPY-863

Books should be returned on or before the
last date stamped below.

22.

21 OCT 03.

23 DEC 1995

08. NOV 04.

20.

19 SEP 1997

18 NOV 1997

- 3 MAR 1998

7 MAY 1998

24. MAY 99

03. MAY 03.

NORTH EAST of SCOTLAND LIBRARY SERVICE
MELDRUM MEG WAY, OLDMELDRUM

LEOPARD, JOHN

Ships in bottles: a
modeller's guide

WITHDRAWN
FROM LIBRARY

745.36238

243301

243301

SHIPS IN BOTTLES
A MODELLER'S GUIDE

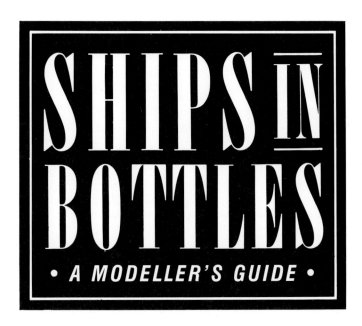

SHIPS IN BOTTLES

• A MODELLER'S GUIDE •

John Leopard

BLANDFORD

Blandford
An imprint of Cassell
Villiers House, 41/47 Strand, London WC2N 5JE

Copyright © John Leopard 1990

All rights reserved. This book is protected by copyright.
No part of it may be reproduced, stored in a retrieval system,
or transmitted in any form or by any means, electronic,
mechanical, photocopying or otherwise,
without written permission from the publishers.

First published 1990

745.36238
243301

British Library Cataloguing in Publication Data
Leopard, John
    Ships in bottles: a modeller's guide.
    1. Model ships in bottles. Construction
    I. Title
    745.5928

    ISBN 0-7137-2138-3

Distributed in the United States by
Sterling Publishing Co., Inc.,
387 Park Avenue South
New York, NY 10016-8810

Distributed in Australia by
Capricorn Link (Australia) Pty Ltd
PO Box 665, Lane Cove, NSW 2066

Typeset by Nene Phototypesetters Ltd, Northampton
Printed and bound in Great Britain by
Courier International, Tiptree, Essex

Contents

Preface

The enthusiastic modeller strives endlessly for perfection and is his own harshest critic. Long after he has impressed the viewer with the quality of his work he seeks to increase his skill, and hence personal pleasure, in the production of still finer models. For this reason, books on modelling aimed solely at the beginner, of which there are many, are of limited usefulness. I have tried to provide a guide that, while explaining every aspect of the modelling process clearly enough to meet the needs of a complete novice, will also be useful to more experienced modellers, who are seeking to improve their techniques. To this end I have pointed out potential pitfalls and have discussed design considerations in enough depth to allow the reader to abandon the examples in Part III and work independently. Using this book a reader with limited experience could make a simple model in seven or eight hours; a more experienced modeller might spend ten times as long producing a full-rigged ship, carrying canvas of forty sails. Whichever project you attempt, take encouragement from the thought that once completed your work could, with luck, remain undisturbed for centuries!

Hayling Island   *John Leopard*

Acknowledgements

A clipper under full sail is one of the loveliest, and now one of the rarest, sights on the sea. The sailors who worked them were proud, as all sailors are, of their ship, and many made models or mementoes of them. Those with an eye for fine detail and miniaturization designed their models to be, miraculously, in full sail within the impossible confines of a bottle. To their example, working with the most basic of tools and on a heaving ship, I owe my inspiration. If they could do it, how much easier it should be for me, I argued, in the comfort of a well equipped workroom.

Before I began my modelling, I read every book I could find about sailing ships, studied models of all shapes and sizes in every maritime museum, and talked to any mariner or modeller who could help. I owe them all my thanks.

Modelling is a solitary pursuit – as, I have discovered, is writing a book. My wife, given every reason to complain, offered instead her endless support and care. It made all the difference. My most sincere thanks are given to my wife Audrey.

Introduction

Model-making, with its wide variety of subjects, provides one of the most relaxing of practical leisure pursuits. There is seldom any pressure to complete a particular model within a specified period and since even the briefest time spent on it during an otherwise busy week will show some progress, few of us can honestly say, 'Oh, I have no time for such a hobby.' Alas, the people most likely to make this statement are often those most in need of the relaxation that modelling can provide. It is also a pity that many people believe themselves to lack even the small skills needed for the easier forms of model-making. In fact, very few of us are completely lacking in manipulative ability.

Nowadays a start can be made with one of those very various and beautifully moulded plastic assembly kits. They demand the minimum of skill while teaching the most valuable of lessons: the need for care and patience. The modeller soon learns that time spent on cleaning up the individual mouldings, the colouring of awkward components before assembly and an orderly progression of work towards completion, all contribute to a more professional and satisfying end result.

The skills needed for putting sailing vessels into bottles are somewhat greater than those required for the assembly of plastic kits but negligible when compared with those needed to manufacture the incredible complex mod-

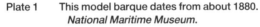

Plate 1   This model barque dates from about 1880.
National Maritime Museum.

Plate 2   Two ships, seven masts, in a single bottle,
date unknown. *National Maritime Museum.*

els of railway engines, men-of-war etc. that grace many of our museums. Take heart from the thought that the original boat-bottlers were the horny-handed seamen from the great days of sail, working with the simplest materials and tools. They had no access to comfortable workshops but had to accomplish their self-imposed tasks wherever space allowed, frequently on the foredeck, where there was more seclusion but also more motion, which would have increased the difficulty of their more delicate operations. A well-sharpened clasp knife would have served for all the carving. The tiny holes (more than a hundred on some of the more detailed models) were probably drilled with a needle twirled between finger and thumb, its point ground to a triangular section to provide cutting edges. Strands of yarn and scraps of the finest cloth they could find completed their resources. Yet they produced some very fine models – often lacking the

delicacy that can be achieved nowadays with superior equipment, but every bit as magical. It would be interesting to know more about these early craftsmen but historians have little to say on the subject and cannot even be sure when the hobby started. Some say that a model in a rather dull green bottle, with cracked paintwork and yellowed sails, might date back to the late eighteenth century. Of course, such an item might also have been produced by a clever modeller who had laid hands on an antique bottle! Any genuine model from that era, however, would feature a shallow-hulled vessel since the deeper-hulled and more interesting ships were too difficult to pass through the bottle neck. With the facilities we now have it is far easier to produce bottled models of galleons, eighteenth-century men-of-war, etc. By the nineteenth century bottle glass tended to be clearer and the beautiful lines of contempor-ary vessels provided the modeller with an exciting challenge. Even so, the models produced do not always match up to the workmanship of older, less elaborate examples. Perhaps some modellers were more interested in providing a conundrum than in producing a finely made model.

If the old salts whose ingenuity produced the best results could see some of the short-cuts practised today, they would be saddened by this degradation of their art. Glass-cutters are sometimes used to cut off the neck or base of the bottle to simplify insertion, and the tell-tale ring is then concealed with a belt of fancy rope-work. Yet nowadays, with the wealth of materials and tools available to us, it is possible to produce – with patience and without recourse to such tricks – ships in bottles the accuracy of which would astound the old shellbacks. Another sad feature of the craft in our times is those catchpenny models one finds in seaside gift shops, whose stark simplicity of design has eliminated all trace of authenticity.

If this book does no more than improve the critical faculties of the reader, I shall feel it has served a good purpose. But my first aim is to help the practitioner by revealing, with the aid of illustrations, the ways to successful modelling. For the benefit of the more experienced I have given detailed consideration to design, encouraging him or her to attempt true-scale models. For the beginner there are a number of exemplary plans to follow in Part III, but as the design work is so important, and an understanding of the way that good design will facilitate the construction of a model even more so, I suggest that whatever your previous modelmaking experience you begin at the beginning and work your way through.

I have just one word of advice to offer the beginner, which the experienced modeller will probably already take for granted, on his tools. There is no reason to use any but the simplest of tools, although you may find marginal advantage to be had from more sophisticated or purpose-made ones. However, they must be razor sharp, and kept so, or replaced as soon as they start to blunt. They have to do delicate work, and you have to avoid the ever present danger of splitting the wood and ruining your model. Most woods are easy enough to work with sharp tools, and common deal or pine will do perfectly well for your hull, but if you are unused to working in fine detail with wood, or have nothing more than a sharp knife to work with, you may find it easier to use balsa wood, an extremely soft medium (but nevertheless a hard wood!) which can be cut and shaped to great precision with a clean, sharp blade.

Beginner or not, I hope to encourage you to develop your skills to the point where you can design and build your own models. Only then can you achieve the satisfaction of honestly being able to say of your model: 'All my own work!'.

Part I

THE DESIGN PROCESS

Good modelling can only begin with good design. It took me many years of trial and error to build up not just the fundamentals of good modelling design, but the numerous 'tricks of the trade' that are so crucial to the quality of the finished ship in a bottle. Part I therefore offers an easy way into acquiring real skills. Who knows what further steps the enthusiast may then be able to take for himself?

1
Preliminary Planning

A newcomer to ship-bottling will probably not wish to make a close study of design and selection problems until he has had a go at something straightforward and satisfied himself that everything really does work. If this is your case, pass fairly swiftly over the next few sections, reserving them for closer attention later, and move on to Parts II and III. However, to maintain a logical sequence of operations I shall consider design first.

The first requirement, and it is surprisingly easy to build up, is a collection of photographs, drawings, plans and other illustrations of sailing vessels. Useful wall charts are available showing side elevations of sailing ships through the ages. There are countless books on the history of sail, often containing just the sort of illustrations the modeller needs. There is no need to hurry your preliminary planning. After all, modelling should be a pleasurable and relaxing activity, as well as a creative process, so take time, as I did, to study the models (sometimes even the original ships) in maritime museums around the country. Make notes of colours, deck fittings, masts and spars, rigging, flags

Plate 3   Schooner with a handsome sheer – see page 86.

and any other interesting features. On the spot sketches and, where practicable, photography may prove a great help later on. Talk to the Curator about his charges. He will enthuse about details you may not have noticed. There is always so much to learn. I was very recently studying those incredible model boats made from bones by French prisoners in the early nineteenth century, when I was told by one of the museum staff that the remarkable fine rigging on one of the smaller boats was made from human hair. Now *there's* an inspiration for the modeller!

Museums are a good source of picture postcards of sailing vessels. Full sail portraits complement side elevations, perhaps obtained from other sources, and help you decide on the finished appearance you want for your model. All sorts of reference material, fun to collect and building up over the years into an invaluable modeller's resource, can be used as a basis for design, but as the finished model will be very small you will need to focus on the sort of detail that establishes identity, not aim for the precision of detail achieved by the larger-scale model manufacturer.

There are three basic aspects to design accuracy:

1 The hull profile must be correct, particularly the bow and stern shapes and the sheer of the deck or decks.
2 The relative heights of the masts and the length of the other spars must be accurate.
3 The number and shape of the sails should follow the original as closely as practical, although some liberties are necessary here to facilitate bottling.

Deck fittings, certain complex arrangements of mast bracing and many other minor details such as figure-heads, decorations and gun ports are of secondary consideration on a small-scale model. Even so, some guidance is given in later sections (pp. 40–41), since it is surprising how much of this detail can be incorporated as the modeller's skill grows. One of the most fascinating aspects of this craft lies in discovering ways to create more exact models.

Since the designer is attempting to produce a readily recognizable model, the degree of accuracy will depend very much upon the original's character. If for instance the subject is the SS *Great Britain*, then its six rather short masts and prominent smoke stack will suffice to identify it immediately, even if other details are far from accurate. A barquentine, on the other hand, is not simply a three-masted vessel with a mixture of square and fore-and-aft sails. Here, where there are several similar types of boat, greater attention to detail is required for accurate identification. In the case of a gift to a friend of his own yacht in a bottle, punctilious attention to detail is necessary if it is not to be taken for another yacht by the same maker or one of almost the same design. Incidentally, a friend's yacht may appeal to a beginner as a project, but would prove difficult because of the delicate carving required and the need to provide many small fittings, such as pulpits, ventilators and so on. Also yachts lack the generous rigging which is the most attractive feature of bottled ships, and are thus rather unrewarding subjects.

2
Fundamental Design Principles

The design of the vessel will in some respects depend on the method of insertion. There are at least three such methods, each with variations and combinations, and no doubt others can be devised.

The first, of which no further mention will be made, is the one touched upon previously: the model can be completed outside and then passed into the bottle through a large hole made by cutting off its bottom. This can subsequently be repaired and the join camouflaged. Whilst the model can be crowded with detail and immaculately finished, I can see little reason for pride in such an achievement. Why not forget the bottle and mount the model on a display stand?

The second method is to construct the vessel with masts set into holes in the deck and hence needing no rigging to support them. The vessel can be dismantled after build and introduced into the bottle piecemeal. Sails, usually cut and shaped in convenient groups, can then be stuck into position. In this case you must forego one of the attractions of all models of sailing ships, irrespective of size or presentation: their remarkable and frequently complex network of rigging. A model built by this method will almost certainly be devoid of rigging, or nearly so. It is no doubt possible to achieve a degree of simulation. Perhaps there is a modeller so skilled that he could devise a method of threading all the rigging, even with the ship already mounted in the bottle.

The rewards for such talent would be small and the results almost certainly less satisfactory than those achieved by the third method, which is the subject of this book.

This method involves completing the model on a build stand outside the bottle but so arranging the spars that they can be collapsed with the sails tidily bundled round them to form a sausage that can be introduced through the bottle neck. The spars can then be re-erected by pulling on appropriate threads which have been left long enough to trail back through the neck. Masts are held rigidly in position during build and after re-erection by standing rigging, i.e. those items of rigging which play no part in the hoisting, furling or control of the sails, but whose function is to support the fixed spars and which, once set up, remain fixed. Figure 1 illustrates the principle. The remaining rigging, not shown in figure 1, plays no part in the raising and lowering of the masts but adds realism to the finished model.

Clearly, if the mast is to collapse, it cannot be set in a hole in the hull; the foot must be free. This feature can be introduced in one of two ways. For the modeller's first attempt, the easiest way is to have a hinge passing through the foot of the mast. This can't be concealed, small though it is, so a little realism is lost. A second method is to locate the rounded foot of the mast in a dimple in the deck (see pp. 57–58 for a description of both methods).

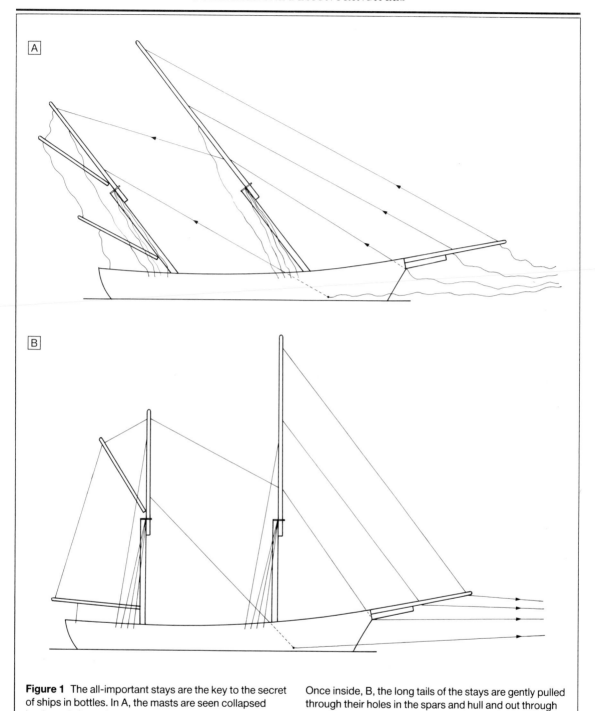

Figure 1 The all-important stays are the key to the secret of ships in bottles. In A, the masts are seen collapsed backwards into a 'sausage', prior to the model being inserted into the bottle.

Once inside, B, the long tails of the stays are gently pulled through their holes in the spars and hull and out through the neck of the bottle to hold the rigging upright.

3
The Choice of Bottle

Having decided which model to attempt, the first thing to do is to relate the scale of the model to the size and shape of the chosen bottle. As those who pursue this hobby find out there is a vast range of bottles available. Any bottle chosen should be as free as possible of distorting irregularities and made from clear glass. (One sometimes sees models in tinted bottles which, in my view, detracts from their attractiveness.)

If you select a flat-sided bottle you can avoid much additional work in the manufacture of a display stand. The proportions of the bottle should as far as possible suit the proportions of the model to be inserted. If a small diameter bottle is chosen for a high-masted ship, it would so reduce the scale of the model that little pleasure would be found in the finished result. On the other hand, if such a vessel as the SS *Great Britain* is made, then its considerable length compared with the mast heights makes the standard wine bottle an ideal choice. The proportions of a Dimple Haig whisky bottle are ideal for most vessels of the two- or three-master square-rigged family. Most of the available space can be filled, the bottle is of pleasing shape and is self-standing. Small wonder that these bottles (no longer as available as they used to be) are sought after by bottleshippers.

When the desire for ever-increasing detail manifests itself, the modeller will need somewhat larger bottles than standard. Unfortunately, many of these have neck sizes which are no greater than their smaller counterparts and therefore allow little scope for increasing the size or detail of the model. There are advantages in slightly larger-necked bottles, however, when vessels with bulky hulls, such as galleons or the massive men-of-war of Nelson's day are being planned (see p. 26).

Bottles with interesting shapes and odd-sized necks can be picked up in antique shops from time to time – but inspect them carefully for distorting irregularities in their manufacture. (Remember, too, that using a wide-necked bottle for a ship that could easily fit through a smaller neck removes some of the fascination of the finished model.)

When I decided to build the *Cutty Sark* under its full canvas of forty sails, I was faced with the problem of finding a suitable bottle. I eventually decided upon a nicely shaped cider flask, sometimes known as a pottle, which is not overlarge but requires mounting. It has a neck which is wide enough to accept a bulky sausage and the completed model fills the available space.

A final consideration when selecting a bottle is the angle of your model's bowsprit and its position relative to the neck of the bottle (see figure 2). Since most of the stays that are used to erect the masts pass through the bowsprit or ship's stem, these two factors will influence the ease or difficulty you will have when it comes to erecting your model.

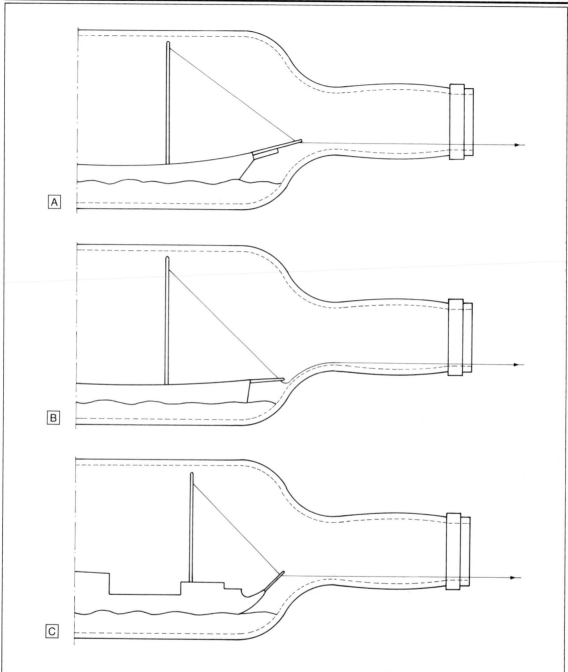

Figure 2 Bottles must be carefully selected to suit the position and attitude of the bowsprit; the bottle should always be chosen to suit the model, rather than the model to suit the bottle. Here, A and C allow unimpeded access for the stay or stays coming through the bowsprit, whereas B is awkward to work, and therefore unsuitable. A bottle with an offset neck, such as a dimple Haig, would be more appropriate for this model.

Plate 4   This well balanced topsail schooner sits neatly in its bottle displaying sails, spars and rigging in perfect proportion.

4
Measuring out the Model

The vessel to be modelled has been decided upon and a suitable bottle has been selected. Design work can start. It is most unlikely that your photograph or drawing of the chosen boat will be to the precise scale required, so the scantlings will require scaling, usually down, to produce a plan for a model that will neatly fit the available space.

First measure the internal diameter of the bottle. To do this, cut a piece of stick to what you judge to be the approximate size. Introduce it into the bottle and with a pair of long tweezers, or wire tongs, manipulate it across the bottle. If it is too short, you can usually judge the extent of the clearance. If it is too long snip a bit off and try again. Having obtained a stick of the correct length, cut half an inch from it to allow for the 'sea' which will be laid in the bottle later. Next lay the stick on the reproduction of the vessel from which you are working and judge the percentage difference between the length of the stick and the height from the water-line to the top of the highest mast in the picture. It is best to do this as accurately as possible, so check your judgement, (an invaluable exercise, you will find, as so much of what you do later has to be done by judgement, or 'eye', rather than by precise measurement, where measurement is frankly impossible) in this instance by measuring both the length of the stick and the waterline to mast top height of your base picture to the nearest millimetre, using a transparent millimetre ruler, then calculate the percentage difference by dividing the difference by the length of the base

height – A in figure 3 – and multiplying by 100. If you don't fear the scorn of ancient mariners a calculator comes in handy at this point!

Now you have the percentage differences for height, apply the same percentage difference to the overall length of the ship and make sure this properly scaled measurement is not too long for the bottle. Height usually dictates the maximum size of the model, but if your rough check suggests that the length is more critical, then check again more carefully and, if need be, base your working drawing on the available length rather than the available diameter of the bottle. The foregoing may sound fussy, but if the object is to produce a correctly scaled model to occupy the maximum available space, then all guesswork should be eliminated. The least troublesome way of producing a scaled-down (or scaled-up) working drawing from the original illustration is to make a measuring card (see figure 3). The card should be 1 in (25 mm) or so taller than the original illustration from which you will be making your model, and 2 or 3 in (up to 75 mm) longer. Draw a base line across the bottom of the card, making sure you have it at right angles to the vertical, and mark the left edge of the card at regular intervals of anything between ¼ in (6 mm) and ½ in (13 mm); experience will show what size spacing you find easiest to work with. Then draw straight lines from each left edge point to converge on the base line where it meets the right hand edge of the card. In figure 3, scale A represents the

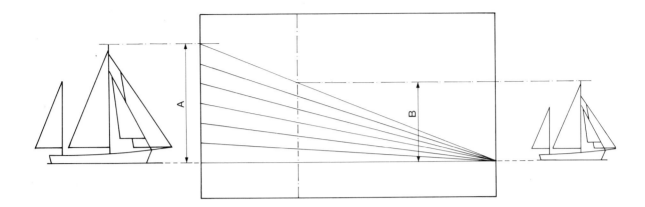

maximum height of the masts on the original, and scale B is marked off across the tapering scale lines at a point where their height is equal to the length of the measuring stick. Cut the card at this point and you have a tool which will save the labour of doing a percentage calculation for every dimension you take from the original reproduction. Clearly, the reduction from scale A to scale B is based entirely on mast height, waterline to top. Any dimension taken from the original drawing, say the hull length, or the spacing of the masts, or even the depth of the bow, should be measured with the A scale and reproduced with the B scale on the working drawing. I cannot stress too much that once the

Figure 3 A scale card is the easiest way to convert a source illustration A into a scaled working drawing. Cut the card from top to bottom at the point where the converging lines are exactly the height of your model, from waterline to topmast, B, and every element of the original design can be reproduced in your drawing to the correct proportion.

sea is in the bottle, the critical overall height of the vessel from sea level to mast head must be checked at every stage. It is desirable to take maximum advantage of the depth available between the surface of the sea and the top of the bottle, but it will spell disaster if, when you get to that stage, there isn't sufficient height to raise the masts to their full extent inside the bottle.

5

The Sea

Although design must necessarily precede most of the practical work, it is as well to complete the sea base for your model at this stage, and in advance of the detailed design considerations. This allows enough time for the sea to dry out completely before you place your finished model on it and also means that the critical dimension from the surface of the sea to the top of the highest mast can be checked before finalizing these and associated details.

The sea can be made from various materials, according to individual preference, after experimenting. I prefer ordinary window putty, which dries relatively slowly, allowing plenty of time to work the surface up into a pleasing form, and also holds impressions well. This is useful later when, after the hull has been carved, you need to press the hull under-plate (see p. 47) into the sea to make a bed for your ship – an impossible operation, of course, if the surface has already hardened. The surface can be checked with a wire probe from time to time and, if necessary, the drying-out process can be slowed down by corking the bottle.

The first task is to colour your sea. If you are using putty, first pour off any surplus oil from the container since the firmer the mix the easier it is to handle. Some recently manufactured putties retain their stickiness for a long time, in which case you will need to prepare your coloured putty very early and allow extra drying time. Place as much putty as you need into a separate container and work it into a regular consistency, adding small quantities of Prussian blue oil paint until a satisfactory colour has been produced. Now add a little green to modify the shade. Be careful not to overdo the colouring or realism will be lost. If you are intending to produce a model with a wealth of rigging detail you may wish to have furled sails or no sails at all so that the grace of the rigging is not obscured. In this case, your ship may be at anchor and you may wish to produce the rather leaden appearance of shallow harbour water. This is obtained by mixing green with a touch of black and of white paint. Once prepared, your putty must be left to dry out until you can handle it without making a mess on your hands.

Before putting the putty into the bottle, make sure that the latter is clean, dry and the best way up. Most bottles have a seam or other unwanted blemish on them, which should be positioned underneath your model. It is all too easy to start pushing in the putty without noticing these features. If you want to include a permanent record of your work, position a small label (well varnished on both sides to minimize oil staining) giving your name, the date and brief details of the vessel on the inside of the bottle where it will be under the sea.

Build up the pile of putty in its correct position little by little. If the consistency is right it can be rolled into sausages, pushed in and then pressed out with a stiff wire with a suitably rolled end. Alternative tools with long handles and spatula-like ends can readily be devised. Should the putty be somewhat

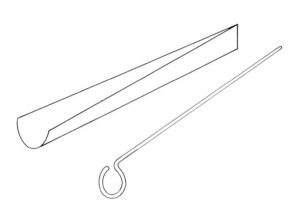

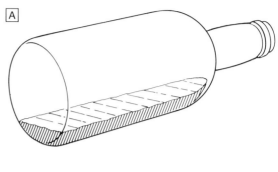

Figure 4 Simple tools to position the putty into the bottle; scoop with a length of partly rolled tin, flattened at one end to form a handle, and push with a shaped piece of wire. Variations on the wire tool will be helpful when you come to position final details on the model, once in the bottle.

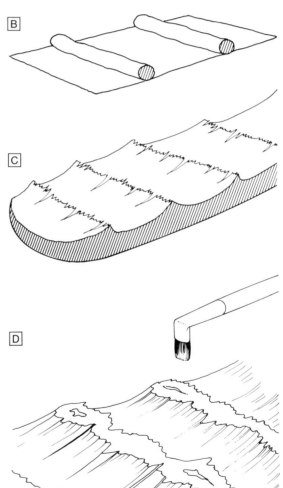

softer it will be necessary to use a scoop and pusher. The scoop can be made from a length of tin rolled into a semi-tube and the pusher from a stiff wire (from a wire coat-hanger, for example) with one end suitably rolled (see figure 4).

It is impossible to avoid staining the inside of the bottle neck but these stains can easily be wiped off with a swab soaked in white spirit or turpentine. Smears further inside the bottle are harder to deal with, so try not to make any. Turpentine and similar agents are unsuitable for use in this case because any that runs onto the putty base will cause stains to seep up the glass.

Spread the putty evenly over the bottom of the bottle, always working outwards to maintain a crisp line around the edge of the sea. Put in sufficient putty to cover the entire

Figure 5 (*right*) A uniform layer of putty, A, makes a calm, flat sea. Add rolls of putty, B, to work into wave shapes, C, breaking the crests with a sharp-ended piece of wire. Paint on the 'white horses', gentle flecks of white, with a right-angled brush, D, once you have the waves looking the way you want them.

24

bottom part of the bottle – it should fill the space as if it were a liquid. In a round bottle the depth in the centre should be about ½ in (13 mm). It is well worth using sufficient putty to achieve this effect, for a well-laid and well-modelled sea adds much to the pleasing illusion of the finished work.

Now the surface of the sea can be roughened to simulate waves. A further piece of that invaluable coat-hanger wire with a short right-angled bend at the business end serves this purpose well but, here again, the enthusiast will develop his own favourite tools. In normal conditions waves do not rise at random but run in a succession of irregular crests and troughs at right angles to the wind. For reasons that will become apparent later, it is best to have the wind blowing from the starboard quarter (i.e. if in the plan view of the bottle the ship is heading towards 12 o'clock, the wind would be blowing from 4 or 5 o'clock). As the waves are drawn up into shape, there may be a tendency for the crests to cling to the tool and leave a broken edge as contact is lost. This is all to the good as it helps produce a convincing appearance of broken foam. Should you have any difficulty in drawing up the wave forms, an alternative method is to lay sausages of putty on the sea in appropriate formation and blend them into the original surface to give the desired crests and troughs.

Now flatten out the central area of waves to receive the hull pattern (see p. 47), after which you can make the final touches. Take a small flat artist's brush with the end bent over and add the wave crests and other areas of broken water with touches of white paint – being sparing except around the area where the hull will rest, particularly at the bow and in the wake of the vessel, where you can be a bit more generous (see figure 5).

6

The Hull – Design Considerations

The side elevation of your model should faithfully follow the profile of the original. In particular, observe the shape of the bow and stern, variations in deck level and the sheer (the general curvature of the deck line). The freeboard (the height of the hull above the water-line) occasionally causes a problem. In most cases the small scale of the vessel gives a freeboard well within the limits imposed by the diameter of the bottle neck, but if it is much above half this diameter there will not be enough space above the deck-line to accommodate the sausage formed by the bundle of masts and sails. It is as well to note at this point that if your vessel has vertical sides, you may need to taper them inwards a little so that the hull and mast assembly can sit lower in the neck of the bottle as it passes through.

Certain high-sided ships, such as galleons with their towering after decks or the multi-gun-decked capital ships of the late eighteenth and early nineteenth century, pose a special problem. Such a hull cannot possibly be squeezed through the neck of a bottle as a single piece, so must be built up as a sandwich. The lower parts of the hull are positioned on the sea bed first, then the top slice, with the sausage of spars and sails, is glued to it. The slicing can be done in two ways. The hull can be made in one piece and sawn into lamina on completion. This method has two snags. First, allowance must be made for the loss of height caused by the wastage of the saw cut, and secondly, this same loss will spoil the fit wherever there is any departure

from the vertical, particularly at bow and stern. The second, and better, method is to build up the parent block from strips of wood and so carve the hull with the divisions already there (see p. 48 for more detail). At this, the design stage, you need to decide on the lamina thicknesses. Since the lower sections will not be encumbered with 'the sausage', they can be of greater depth than the top section (see figure 6). You will also see that the line of the bottom of the top slice clears the upswept prow on the second slice. This may require a small departure from true scaling. If such a modification departs too far

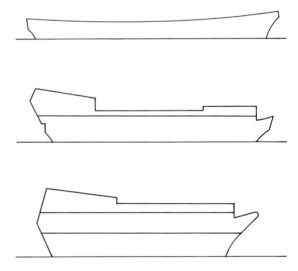

Figure 6 Not every hull shape can pass through the neck of the bottle in one piece. Taller hulls, such as those of the galleon and ship of the line below, can be introduced layer by layer.

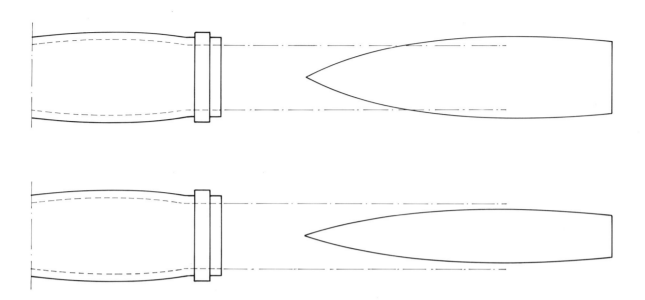

Figure 7 A correctly scaled beam may be too large to pass through the neck, and must be narrowed when planning the model. This is one of a number of compromises to true scale modelling imposed by the size and limitations of the bottle, but in no way does it distract from the beauty of the finished ship.

from the truth, then you will need to add a pimple to the prow as a separate exercise.

A further point to watch at the design stage is the width of the beam: many hulls are surprisingly beamy for their length and this is likely to inhibit entry through the bottle neck. It is scarcely practical to laminate the vessel in the vertical plane, if only because of the arrangement of the rigging, so even the purist will have to resort to a deliberate reduction of the beam (see figure 7). This small infidelity will almost certainly escape notice as once the ship is in the bottle few view points reveal the beam at its true scale, particularly when there is a good spread of canvas. Furthermore, the slight distortion caused by the curvature of the glass tends to compensate by exaggerating the ship's beam.

I would recommend that your earlier projects should involve ships with raised bulwarks, not flush decks. The carving is a little more exacting but the drilling of bulwarks for shrouds and other rigging is so much easier.

Plate 5   This model of a galleon completely fills the space inside its square bottle. The optical qualities of decorative bottles sometimes produce unpredictable effects on spars and rigging.

7
Designing the Spars

Even if it is not always possible to scale the hull precisely because of the limitations imposed by the diameter of the bottle neck, an accurate profile is essential for a realistic effect. This means precise positioning and correct height and angle of the spars. You will notice that the masts of all large ships are constructed from two or more sections, a feature that must be reflected in your design (see pp. 82–92). It pays to check the development of the design at all stages of production. In particular, check mast heights after the sea is in and the hull has been carved, for a mast that is the merest fraction too long will foul the side of the bottle.

Spars fall into four main categories:

1 Masts
2 Yards (the horizontal spars which carry the square sails)
3 Booms and gaffs (the spars that carry the fore and aft sails)
4 Bowsprits and jib-booms (the spars which project beyond the bow and provide a means of securing the various stays which support the foremast and up which the triangular headsails are hoisted)

The various minor, or less common spars shown in your original illustration are mostly too small to be incorporated into so tiny a model. Nevertheless, there are some secondary spars which can enhance the grace of the finished model and should be included if possible. The bowsprit shrouds, which inhibit the horizontal movement of this important load carrier, are sometimes made angular by the introduction of minor spars which push them into the new shape, much as the crosstrees on the mast interrupt the straight run of the topmast shrouds. These spars are well worth including, as they add realism to the forward arrangement of the ship. Also associated with the bowsprit is a further but very noticeable spar, which projects from the underside of the bowsprit and is called the dolphin striker, so named, one assumes, because it ends quite close to the surface of the sea and could hit a nearby dolphin if the ship pitched violently. This spar puts an angle into the bobstay in precisely the same way as the crosstrees and bowsprit shroud spreaders put angles into their associated rigging. These minor spars can be seen in figure 22, page 57.

On some earlier galleons a very small mast can be found at the forward end of the bowsprit, carrying a small square sail. Although very minor, and without any immediately obvious practical function, on an appropriate model it is exactly this sort of detail which lends accuracy and realism, and however difficult to design and make really ought not to be omitted.

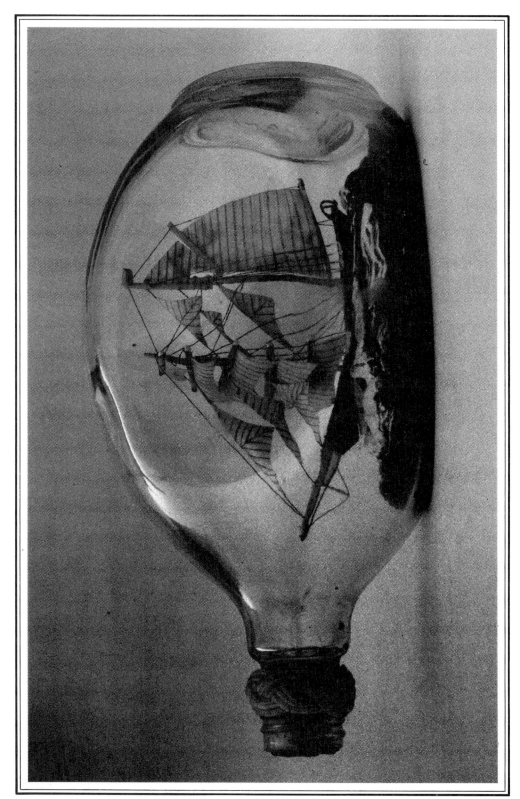

Plate 6   The outline of the author's model brigantine is gracefully matched by the shape of its bottle. Note the detail at the stern end and on the bowsprit.

8
Designing the Rigging

Now that your working drawing has hull and spars, the most fascinating design task remains: the addition of the rigging, by which the masts and bowsprit are held in position. In almost all cases mast rigidity is achieved by bracing in three directions. A pair of shrouds, or in the case of larger vessels probably two sets of shrouds, lead from one or more positions on the mast to either side of the vessel, just aft of the mast, and inhibit forward or sideways movement. A stay, or a series of stays, lead forward from the mast to a more forward mast or to the deck (in the case of the foremast to the bowsprit or stem head) and prevent the mast(s) from falling backwards. The shrouds, which can be added to the working drawing with fair accuracy, should be restricted to no more than four terminating at any one point on the mast and five in total. This is because most of the shrouds will pass through the same hole in the mast, and threading becomes more difficult as their number increases. All of the shrouds pass through holes spread along the gunwale and if these are closer together than say $\frac{3}{32}$ in (2 mm) the wood is likely to split. It is more desirable to reproduce the overall spread of the shrouds along the gunwale accurately than to retain the correct number.

In designing the stays you will need to take certain liberties (see figure 10) since all stays must pass through holes in masts, decks and bowsprit to act as a means of re-erecting the masts once the boat is in the bottle (figure 1). Figure 8 shows a simple arrangement of shrouds and forestay. Figure 10a shows the true layout of the major stays on the *Cutty Sark*. The stays between the masts, if fixed on the model would break during collapse (see figure 9). The possible variations shown in figure 10b give stays that are somewhat out of true position but are simple to run through

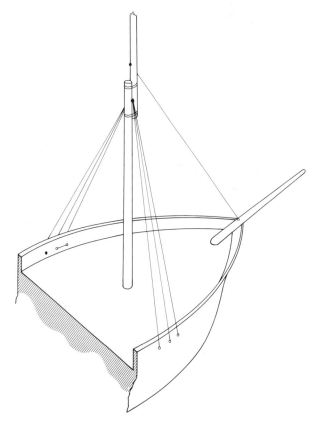

Figure 8 A triangular structure, seen here in its simplest terms, keeps the mast rigid: a stay to the forward, and a set of shrouds to either side. The foot of the mast sits in a hole in the deck. Note the stepped mast, the two parts bound together by thick rope. The topmast is always to the fore of its lower section.

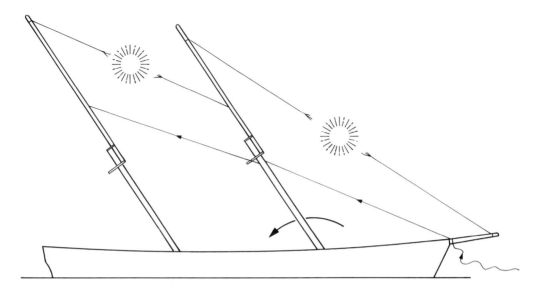

Figure 9 Stays must be free to run through their forward holes (see also figure 1), when the masts are folded back. If not, they will break, or worse, break the masts and spars.

the hull at deck level. The dotted lines indicate an alternative, more nearly correct position, which although it produces a redundant stay forward of each mast, allows a better arrangement of staysails. Figure 10 also shows a minor adjustment to the position of one of the yards on the mizen mast, so that it falls opposite the gaff. By this means one hole only through the mast will serve to secure both spars. (The system of tying off is explained later, pp. 65–67.)

Note that all stays for masts with yards must pass as close as possible to the top side of the nearest yard though the holes for securing yards and stays must not be so close that they splinter into one. If the hole for a stay were to be positioned to reach the mast mid-way between two yards, the stay would pass through a square sail.

Once you have designed the standing rigging that controls the erection of the masts you can add the lesser standing rigging, which in some cases adds stiffness to the masts and bowsprit. Again it may be necessary to make small adjustments to their

terminal points on the masts to avoid placing holes too close to others already planned.

Next the remaining rigging, which on an actual ship controls the setting of the sails, can be added. On the model its chief function is to add realism (see figure 11).

The yards which carry the square sails are set to the correct angle for the wind direction with braces secured to the ends of the yards. For high yards these braces lead to blocks secured to the next mast aft and thence to the deck level for hauling. In the case of the lower yards, the braces lead to blocks at deck level. For the purpose of the model a representation of the braces can be achieved by simply securing a thread to one end of the yard, passing it through a hole in the next mast aft and so back to the other end of the yard. Those which terminate at deck level pass through holes in the gunwales, where they are secured. Here again, as in the case of

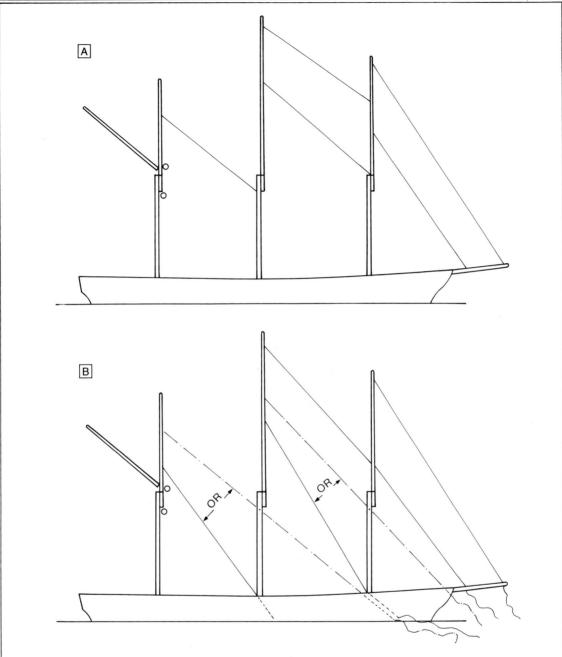

Figure 10 A, above, shows the true arrangement of stays on the ship being modelled. B, below, shows the modifications which must be made if there is to be any chance of getting the model into a bottle. On paper, this looks like a substantial change, but in practise, once the model is finished, it looks perfectly normal. The way you modify the stays may depend, at least in your earlier models, on your skill at drilling running holes through the masts rather than through the hull.

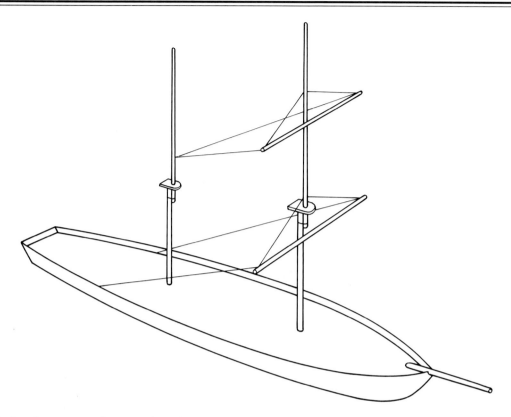

the holes for stays, take care that the holes in the masts are close to the top of the adjacent spar to avoid fouling the sails.

Yards on real ships are adjusted for height by lifts which are secured to the yard end, pass through blocks set higher on the masts, and so back to deck level. In the case of the model, the lifts too simply pass through a hole a little above the yard position. Apart from lending realism to the model, the friction of these threads as they pass through the various holes keeps the yards in their proper places once they have been adjusted after re-erection in the bottle.

This completes the design of the major items of running and standing rigging associated with a square-sailed vessel. A close study of the original will reveal a wealth of other detail, but on a model of this size little

Figure 11 This is a formalized representation of the running rigging which controls the set of the square sails. This arrangement looks realistic, without being functional, since the sails cannot of course be controlled from the deck, as they would be on a working ship. But, as with other compromises we have seen, it does not matter. The important thing is that the model should *look* right. Note again the stepped masts, their joins this time marked by a substantial wooden platform called a top. Three-section masts with two such tops are better modelled in two sections only, as inevitably the thickness of your masts will be out of true scale and unnecessarily emphasized by the second, higher join.

is gained by adding still more to an already crowded plan.

The rigging associated with the fore-and-aft sails (those other than square sails) is much simpler. As a rule the staysails are of triangular form and are normally cleated to the stays. The remaining sails are those

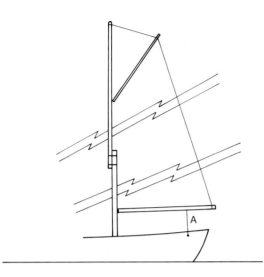

Figure 12 This rigging arrangement maintains the spars of a typical fore and aft rig in their correct relationship. It adds realism, but as in figure 11 is not truly functional. The sheet A used to control the boom is represented in the model simply by a short thread from the boom to the outside of the gunwale on the port quarter.

supported by a spar or spars from the after side of one or more of the masts. These spars need to be maintained in their correct positions by the kind of arrangement shown in figure 12.

The remaining running rigging, the sheets, are used to control the angle of the fore-and-aft sails. Where the sail is attached to a boom it is necessary to simulate sheets simply to steady the boom and maintain the tension on the rest of the associated rigging (see point A,

figure 12). In the case of the staysails, where there is nothing to maintain the tension (lacking a real wind) their inclusion adds nothing to the grace of the model and can be ignored.

Major rigging arrangements apart, as has already been described there are a number of intricate bracing lines associated with the bowsprit which add realism and detail, and will enhance the overall appearance of your model's rigging if you can include them. The sails themselves offer further opportunities to model fine-detail rigging. Most sails, particularly square sails, require a means of reefing them, that is, reducing the amount of sail area in strong winds to keep the vessel under control, without removing the sail entirely. This involves rolling up part of the sail, and securing the roll to the yard by means of one of a series of horizontal rows of short lashings which appear on both sides of the sail and are long enough to be tied together over a yard. These rows of evenly spaced reefing points, with their short lengths of rope trailing out from the surface of the sails, are usually depicted on models with minute pencil strokes on both sides of the sails. However, greater accuracy, and therefore greater effect, can be obtained by passing very short lengths of hair or very fine cotton through the sails and securing them with that invaluable nail varnish. Experimenting with such fine details may well lead you to discover techniques useful in other areas of your model's rigging.

Plate 7   The fifteen sails on this three-masted barque need
a steady hand to pattern and patch them realistically.
The flags add bright colour to the model.

9
Designing the Sails

We are not concerned at this stage with the way in which the sails can be made to achieve a realistic curvature, seams and possibly patches, but simply with their arrangement on the working drawing. In many diagrams of square-riggers, the sails are shown as if the yards are running fore and aft. This is a convenient way of putting a lot of information on one drawing, though clearly it is not the way in which they will set when the model is built. However, when the rigging and the sails all appear on one drawing as small as the one presently being prepared, the result can be confusing. Although the sample drawing on p. 92 of the SS *Great Britain* shows everything on the one drawing, any more complex arrangement needs two separate drawings, as in the case of the barque (pp. 88–90).

Now add all the fore-and-aft sails to the appropriate drawing. The shapes of these will also require a little modification, since the stays on the plan will not necessarily follow the same route as those on the original. Even so, they must be arranged to fill the available space conveniently and present the same graceful shape as the originals. Draw them carefully because later you will trace them for manufacture. For example, the foot of each of the headsails (set fore and aft between the foremast and the bowsprit) will usually be at the same angle to the horizontal. If this is what the original shows, then the model should follow the same plan. Variations can spoil the appearance of the finished model.

Likewise the square sails should show a pleasing gradation from the smallest to the largest. Examples of good and bad practice are given in figure 14 overleaf.

The stays and braces as they pass over the top of (but not too close to) the nearest yard will tend to foul the foot of the next sail up.

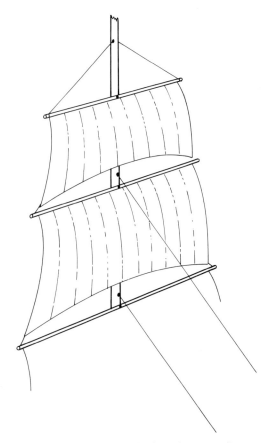

Figure 13 A generous curve at the foot of square sails looks good on the model, but its real purpose is to allow ample clearance for those stays which pass between the sails.

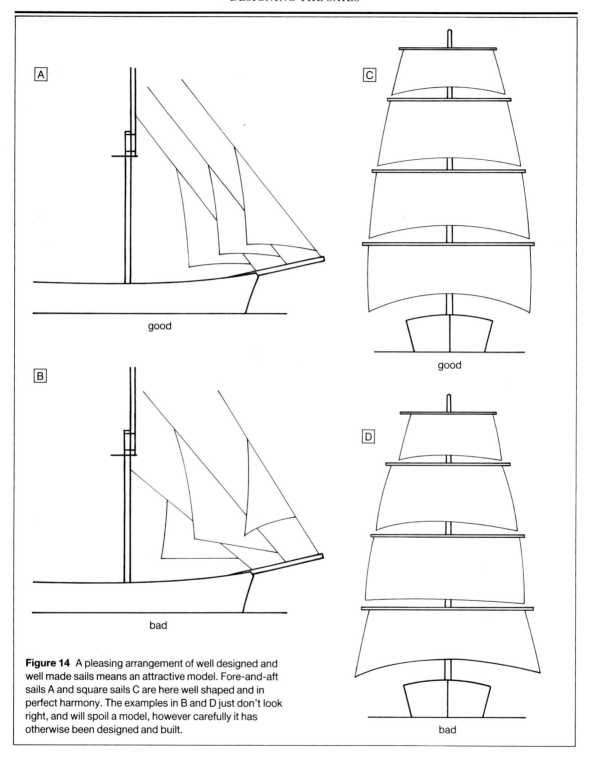

good

bad

good

bad

Figure 14 A pleasing arrangement of well designed and well made sails means an attractive model. Fore-and-aft sails A and square sails C are here well shaped and in perfect harmony. The examples in B and D just don't look right, and will spoil a model, however carefully it has otherwise been designed and built.

You may therefore need to be generous with the curvature at the foot of affected sails – a liberty that improves rather than detracts from the appearance of the sails (see figure 14).

At this stage check the distribution of holes to be drilled through the masts for yards, booms, lifts, braces, shrouds and stays. It is surprising how many there are, some fore-and-aft and some athwartships. Minor adjustments to the design may be necessary to ensure that no group of holes is so crowded that mast strength is seriously impaired. The neatest way to terminate stays at the masts is to draw a glued stopper knot into a hole (see p. 63), but to avoid overcrowding you may need to make a tie instead. If two drillings in opposite directions need to be within $\frac{1}{16}$ in (1 mm) of each other, or drillings in the same plane are within $\frac{3}{32}$ in (2 mm) of each other, then any stays terminating in that area need to be tied around the mast to avoid more drilling.

Most designs for ships in bottles, including those shown in Part III of this book, have all the vessel's sails set and drawing. However, there would have been many times in the original ship's working life when the full set of sails was not in use, and you may want to reflect the practical operation of a sailing ship in your model. Fore-and-aft sails are usually furled (folded up) by lowering the gaff on to the boom and tying the spars and

the sail into a tidy bundle. Foresails are lowered to the deck and bundled up for short periods, or removed altogether for longer times out of use. In strong winds, the topsails are first to be furled, after which the larger sails below are reefed, as we have seen, or furled completely. Sailing ships of war would furl their courses, that is the lower sails on all masts, to give greater visibility from the quarter deck in battle, and to avoid fires on deck. Ships in dock have all their sails furled or stowed away.

You may therefore want to design your model with interesting variations from the full set of sails. A model heeled over a little in the bottle, with reefed and furled sails (see figure 35) and a rough sea, can give a pleasing effect of a ship in strong winds. A model of a ship alongside a jetty, on a completely calm sea, with all its sails furled and the mooring ropes clearly in evidence, gives you the chance to show off extra detail in your rigging and deck fittings.

If you feel adventurous, a model of the brigantine *Mary Celeste*, found deserted at sea with not a soul on board, some few sails set, others torn and blowing in tatters from the yards, others furled and still others in untidy bundles roughly secured at deck level, makes an unusual talking point. Contemporary accounts of her discovery show the state she was in, and provide a good basis for your model.

10
Designing the Deck Fittings

This aspect of your design is likely to lead to the greatest departures from the original. Most vessels have their decks covered with a great many details which could not possibly be reproduced on so small a model.

Those features which can be included fall into two groups: 1) items such as hatch covers or similar objects of little height; 2) bulkier features, the omission of which would remove the character of the model. The former present no difficulties, since they can easily pass through the neck of the bottle. Care must however be taken that hatch covers or other items situated just aft of a mast are not going to impede its collapse at the time of entering the bottle. The vertical scaling of these features may have to be reduced to token thickness only, but a change of colour between them and the deck will give them proper significance.

The bulkier fixtures, such as smoke stacks, bridge assemblies, lifeboats on davits and sizeable deck houses (see figure 15), may add too much to the height or width of the model to make entry into the bottle possible. In such cases these parts of the vessel have to be made separately and added after the model has been re-erected in the bottle (see pp. 76–77).

However, should you choose to present your model with its sails fully furled, it becomes an easier task to introduce more detail on to the deck. Your source illlustrations will give you more than enough ideas of what to include. Capstans, coils of rope, donkey engines, anchor chains, ventilators,

all sorts of sundry equipment, much of which need be only of minimal height, will all add extra interest to the model.

Much can be done with small sections (flat and round) cut from the larger diameter scraps of cocktail sticks, for example, and metal can be simulated with carefully smoothed gold or silver foil. For instance, a ship's boat might be lashed upside down to the deck or on top of a low deck house. A very narrow strip of silver foil glued along the line of the keel will improve it considerably. Lifebelts are easily made from flat coils of white thread, with opposing dabs of red paint, and a low pile of secured deck cargo, timbers perhaps, represented by thin lengths of cocktails sticks.

A realistic capstan can be made from a larger diameter cocktail stick. Hold the stick in the jaws of an electric drill, cut it flat across its widest diameter, and hollow it slightly with a small round file. Remove the stick, and cut it neatly above and below the hollowed out part. Cover the top face with a tiny disc of silver foil, pressed into the hollow, and mark around the top circumference a ring of fine black ink dots. A few turns of cotton around the capstan will look like rope, which you can later lead away from the capstan to two short lengths of wire set into the finished deck, close to each other, to represent bollards. The deck itself will be much improved if 'planked' from stem to stern with fine black lines. Hatch covers may be similarly treated, or painted a contrasting colour and then lined.

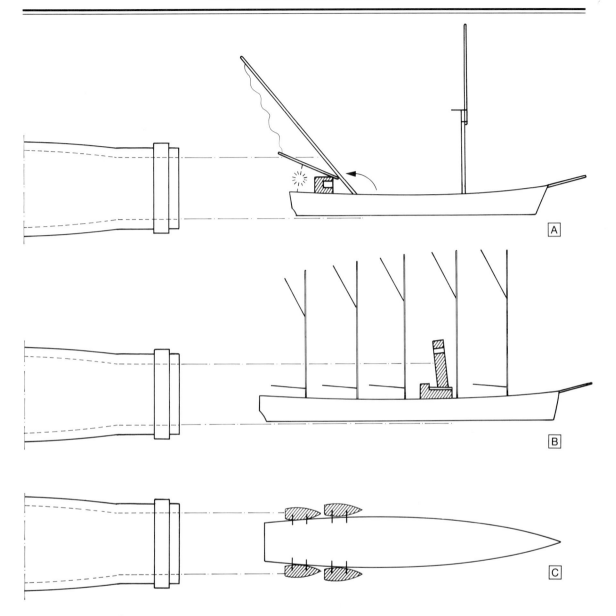

Designing and making the deck fittings is much the same operation. You may find it convenient to design and make those that can be fitted outside the bottle at an early stage, so that your bottling process – the ultimate satisfaction – is not held up at the last minute while you work away at yet more intricate details.

Figure 15 The deckhouse in A, above, will obstruct the lowering of the mast and must therefore be fitted after the ship is in the bottle. The funnel, B, and the lifeboats, C, are likewise too big to be included in the 'sausage' and can only be fitted subsequently. Make sure that your 'sausage' will fit *before* you embark upon the entry.

Part II

THE MODELLING PROCESS

In this section I describe the actual building of a model, using both simple and more involved techniques. It is for the reader to decide upon his or her own limitations. A simple model, nicely presented, is far better than a poorly executed ambitious model or, worse still, one which has to be abandoned before completion. For this reason, one or two of the examples shown at the end of this book are very straightforward. For a beginner the wisest approach is to keep things as simple as possible.

Plate 8   An 'aerial' view of the barque shows up the carved bulwarks and deck detail.

11
Making the Hull

No special wood is required for this purpose. A short length of 2×1 in (50×25 mm) planed deal will serve the purpose, but it should be selected with straight grain and be free from knots. To the lower edge of this workpiece, screw a similar length of say 3×1 in (75×25 mm) wood to form a stand and to provide means of clamping the assembly to the edge of the work bench or table, so that it can be carved at varying angles.

The necessary tools include a tenon saw or similar tool, and a selection of carvers, chisels and whatever other edged tools you find useful.

As mentioned previously, it is a good idea to choose a vessel with raised bulwarks for your first efforts. Whilst the carving is somewhat more exacting, the rigging is easier. Whatever form has been selected and whatever tools are employed, the secret is to carve with very small cuts only, particularly in the opening phases. The task becomes progressively easier as the shape develops.

The raising of the gunwales or, more properly, the lowering of the deck level can be performed with any sharp cutting tool: the combination of a keen point and a carver's chisel with a right-angled cutting edge will produce a clean corner between gunwale and deck. Figures 16a-h overleaf illustrate the usual sequence of operations:

1 Produce a carved plan view of the hull (16a-c)
2 Put sheer (curve) into the top face of the block (16d)
3 Hollow out the area inside the gunwales,

down to required deck level (16e-f). Because of the difficulty of producing a clean corner where the gunwales take a sharp bend across the stern of the ship, a much neater finish can be achieved if the stern piece of the gunwale is omitted altogether at the carving stage and glued into place later as a separate fitting.

When a small hull is being carved on which the gunwales need to be very thin there is a risk of splitting them while carrying out 3) above. It is therefore advisable to adopt another sequence, in which the carving of the plan is the last rather than the first operation.

1 Mark position of bow and stern on top of block, and put in the curve of the sheer.
2 Mark on the hollowed out surface the plan of the vessel with a double line to show the inside and the outside of the gunwales. Now hollow out the area inside the gunwales down to the proper deck level.
3 Finally carve out the plan shape of the vessel. You will be able to make the gunwales as thin as practical without danger of splitting them.

You will notice that the plan of the hull is carved to well below the water-line level, before separation from the parent block. Now scribe in the water-line on the hull with a pencil secured to or held closely to a block cut to the required height, and carefully saw the model off the block. Check its size in the neck of the bottle and adjust if necessary. Next saw a wafer of wood, about 1/8 in (3 mm) thick, below the water-line. After painting

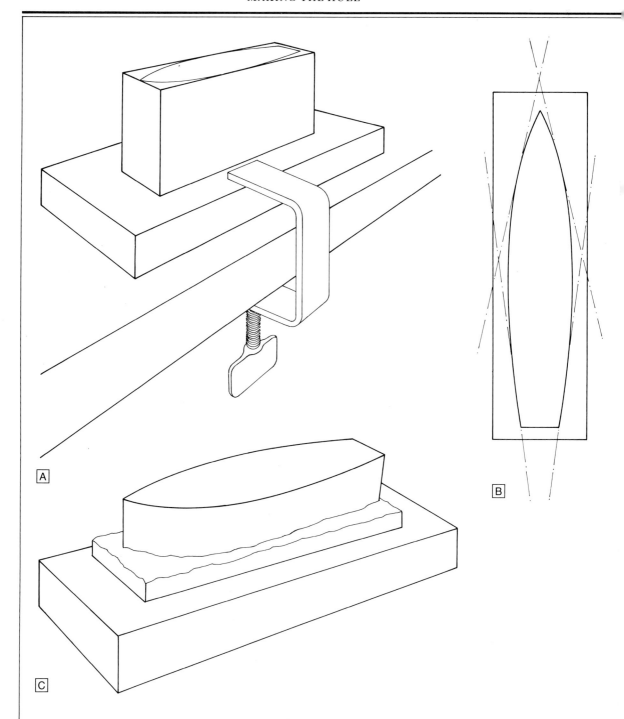

A

B

C

Figure 16 A, The block of wood from which the hull is to be shaped is screwed, from the underneath, to a wooden base piece, which can be clamped to the workbench. B, shows the plan of the hull drawn on the block. The dotted lines indicate the first of the saw cuts. C, Now the carving is complete, from the plan drawing to a point well down the block and below the waterline. D, The fore and aft curvature of the deck – the sheer – and the shaping of the stem and stern of the vessel produce the finished hull shape. At this point, the waterline is scribed around the hull and another

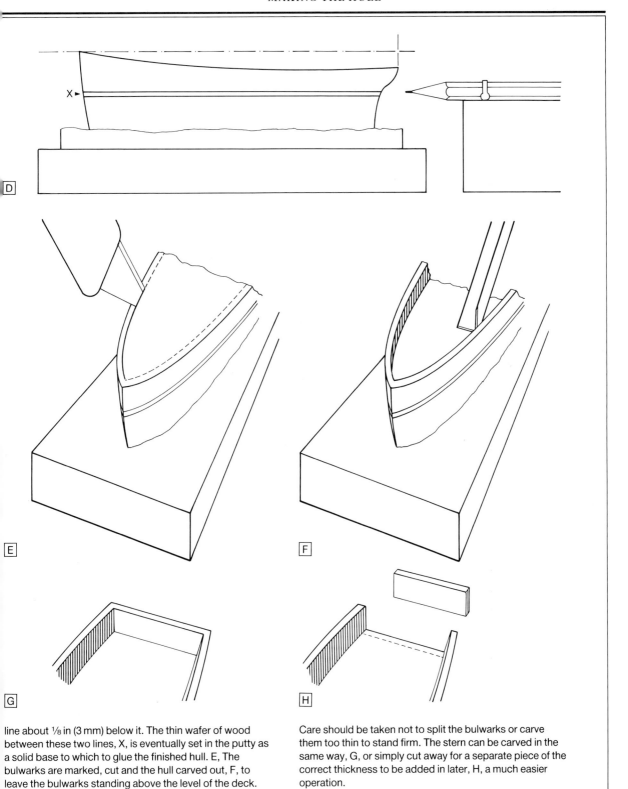

line about ⅛ in (3 mm) below it. The thin wafer of wood between these two lines, X, is eventually set in the putty as a solid base to which to glue the finished hull. E, The bulwarks are marked, cut and the hull carved out, F, to leave the bulwarks standing above the level of the deck.

Care should be taken not to split the bulwarks or carve them too thin to stand firm. The stern can be carved in the same way, G, or simply cut away for a separate piece of the correct thickness to be added in later, H, a much easier operation.

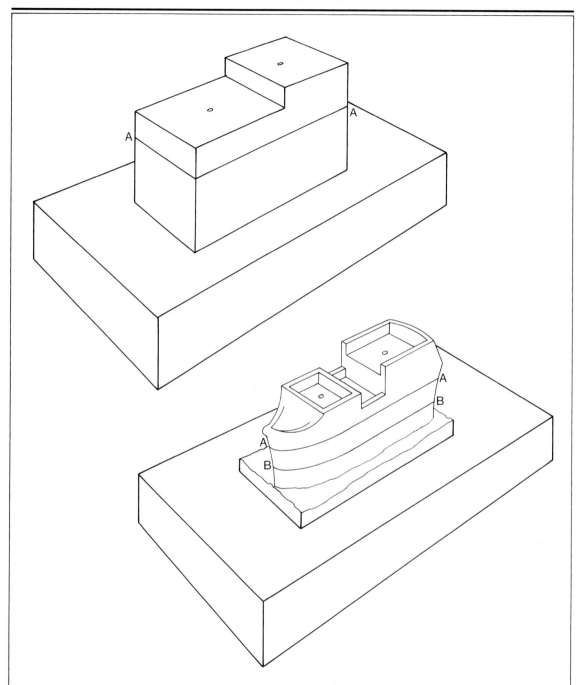

Figure 17 When a hull is too deep to allow easy entry into the bottle it has to be formed from two or more layers screwed together, which can be separated after the carving is complete and introduced into the bottle one by one. (See also figure 6.) Here, a two layered hull is shown screwed together before carving, A, and a three layered hull completed, B, but not yet waterline scribed or cut from its base.

the edges, with an overlap on top, the same colour as that decided for the hull, press it into the sea until it is flush, then place the bottle in a very warm place for final drying out. It is, of course, possible to stick the hull, after insertion, directly upon a flattened area of sea, but the least irregularity impairs the bond or, worse still, you find daylight showing through a gap under some part of the hull.

As explained earlier (pp. 26–27), deep-hulled vessels need to be made in several sections. Screw the lamina together, using fine-gauge screws located where the mast steps will fall, to hold them together for carving. When carving has been completed, plug the screw holes, which will eventually be concealed under the masts (see figure 17), saw the hull from the parent block and transfer it to a build stand (pp. 50–51). Because you will need to paint the hull while it is still on the stand (see pp. 72–73), insert a piece of greaseproof paper between hull and stand-top to keep the latter clean for your next model. Now, screwing through from the underside of the build stand and using screws short enough not to pierce through the decks, fix your hull firmly to the stand.

Once the hull is screwed to the build stand, you will be anxious to get on with the fascinating task of drilling, erecting and securing the masts, bowsprit and rigging.

It is as well to pause before starting this work to consider how the various deck fittings are to be accommodated. This may involve a little extra chisel work on part of the deck (for example, to cut away some space beneath the big skylight on the S.S. *Great Britain*, project 5), or some holes which are simple to drill before the masts are assembled, but certainly more difficult afterwards.

There is one other major consideration at this stage. If holes have to be drilled through the hull at awkward angles, it can sometimes best be done before the hull is cut from its parent block. The possible problems posed by these holes are considered more fully in the next section on the build stand.

49

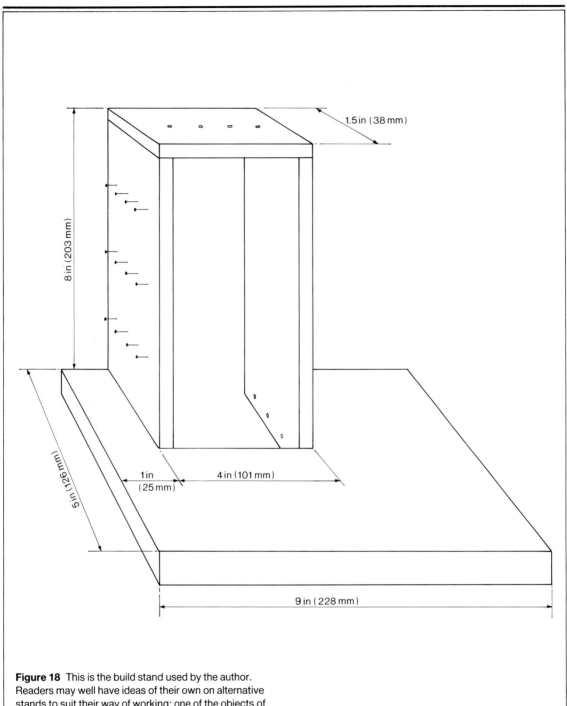

1.5 in (38 mm)

8 in (203 mm)

5 in (126 mm)

1 in
(25 mm)

4 in (101 mm)

9 in (228 mm)

Figure 18 This is the build stand used by the author.
Readers may well have ideas of their own on alternative
stands to suit their way of working; one of the objects of
this book is to encourage modellers to think for themselves
as they extend and develop their skills.

12
The Build Stand

A build stand serves a number of useful purposes. Indeed, without it the task of completing the model once the hull has been carved would be considerably complicated.

1 The model is firmly held and by adjusting the position of the D clamp that secures it to the worktable the modeller has easy access to that part of it on which he is working.

2 The height of the stand places the model conveniently: just below eye level when you are seated at the worktable.

3 It provides a convenient anchoring point for the tails of the stays so that during the build each mast, once made, can be firmly held in its vertical position whilst further spars and sails are added.

4 It provides a work surface for drilling spars and other such odd jobs.

The stand illustrated in figure 18 can be varied to suit the modeller's own ideas but remember that you will need to provide screwdriver access for when you secure your model to the stand (provided in the case illustrated by the cut out in the base). Whilst drawing pins, for example, can provide alternative anchoring points for the tails of the stays, twin panel pins permit easy cleating. Be generous with these pins. Some positions will be found to be more convenient than others, and some of the more complex ships have a surprising number of tails.

The build stand illustrated serves well for all straightforward models, but it is worth considering the requirements of the less usual models, particularly those which have rigging holes running through them at odd angles. One example is shown in figure 29. There is no difficulty in drilling these holes, but the problem arises when the needle which carries the rigging thread finds insufficient clearance below the hole before it strikes the top of the build stand and is stuck half in and half out of the hole. In such cases it is helpful to introduce a piece of wood which is no more than the beam of the hull in width, but deep enough to allow needle clearance, between the hull and the top of the build stand. Clearly you should use the shortest needles available, so that the filler piece need not be unduly deep.

Alternatively, the width of the top of the build frame can be reduced from 1½ in (38 mm) down to as little as ½ in (12 mm), but at the risk of weakening the frame considerably and inviting wholly damaging failure at an advanced stage of your model's construction. If you have two models on the go at the same time, or are enthusiastic enough to start a new model as soon as the last one if finished, you can experiment with two different build stands, designed to cover all eventualities.

Plate 9   The topsail schooner sits neatly in its bottle displaying sails, spars and rigging in perfect proportion.

13
Making the Spars

Cocktail sticks provide convenient timbers for masts and most other spars, but are a little too thick so require sanding down. This can best be done by holding the stick in the jaws of an electric drill and rubbing it with a piece of folded sandpaper held between finger and thumb. It is a matter of experiment and judgement to decide by how much the stick can be reduced before it becomes too thin for drilling. Since yards are drilled in the centre only, these can be tapered a little so that the outer ends are more delicate. This minor departure from fact improves the appearance of the finished model.

The very light spars that can be fitted without any drilling can be made from stiff broom bristles or from tiny twigs from hedgerows. The straight dry radiating stems which support the florets of cow parsley blooms are particularly useful. These light spars can be used, in a more ambitious model, to carry the stunsails, which extend beyond normal square sails on ships such as Clippers which carry so imposing a spread of canvas (see figure 19). Broom bristles make excellent flag staffs and have the added advantage of being springy enough to bend out of the way when passing through the neck of the bottle.

The best drill for making the numerous holes required in hull and spars is a Number 64 twist drill, which is about the size of a darning needle. Some slightly smaller should be obtained for particularly thin mast heads and some a little larger for points where lower and upper masts join, so that a larger

hole can be drilled to accommodate the numerous shrouds spreading from this point.

Before drilling, each spar must be cut and shaped. A convenient way of keeping them together is to attach each one to the working drawing, in its correct position, with a small blob of Blu-Tack (malleable, reusable, plasticine-like adhesive). To those who are unfamiliar with this useful compound, it is an easily-worked, non-drying plastic material with adhesive qualities that will grip most substances and can be rolled off after use, leaving little or no mark. It can be used over and over again if not exposed to too much air or heat and is obtainable from most stationers.

Drilling items as small as spars presents a

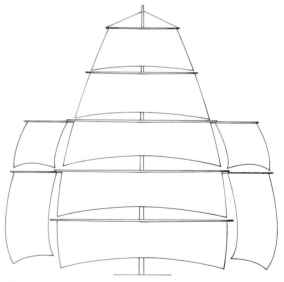

Figure 19 Square sail yards are sometimes extended to include stunsail yards, but a model with stunsails will need a big bottle with a bigger neck diameter than usual.

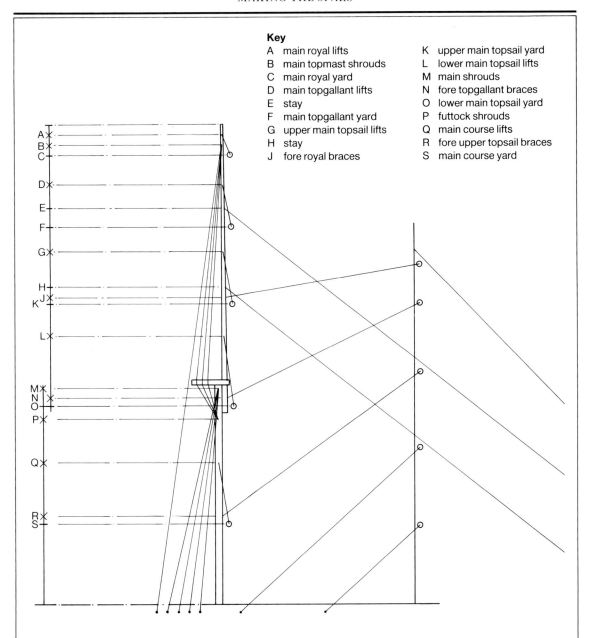

Key

A	main royal lifts	K	upper main topsail yard
B	main topmast shrouds	L	lower main topsail lifts
C	main royal yard	M	main shrouds
D	main topgallant lifts	N	fore topgallant braces
E	stay	O	lower main topsail yard
F	main topgallant yard	P	futtock shrouds
G	upper main topsail lifts	Q	main course lifts
H	stay	R	fore upper topsail braces
J	fore royal braces	S	main course yard

Figure 20 Complex rigging structures demand careful drilling of the masts, and a drilling plan will ensure that the right holes are put in the right places. Draw the mast and rigging, actual size, and at every point where the rigging must go through the mast, extend a horizontal line to the edge of your drawing. Mark the position of fore and aft holes with horizontal strokes, as shown, and transverse holes with crosses. When you are ready to drill, lay the marked edge of the drawing against the mast, and carefully mark drilling points and directions. It is as well to draw up a plan like this for every mast that requires multiple drilling. Note that drillings for stays and braces must be just above the nearest yard to provide sail clearance.

holding problem. A most satisfactory way of resolving this is to spread a thin layer of Blu-Tack over a small area of drilling board – the base of the build stand will serve very well – and then press the spar to be drilled into this coating. It will be held sufficiently firmly for marking, centring and drilling to proceed without trouble.

A model ship contains many drilled holes, some in almost concealed positions. Some of these pass fore and aft through the mast, others pass athwartships. Where the upper and lower mast junction forms a step, a lip must be provided for fore-and-aft drillings. Several movements of the work piece may be necessary to complete all this. It is very easy to overlook the drilling of a hole and discover this only late in assembly of the model. It pays, therefore, with all but the simplest masts, to draw a drilling guide for each mast (see figure 20) using a strip of paper which can be laid alongside the mast to be drilled, both as a check and a scale. Fore-and-aft holes can be indicated with strokes and transverse holes with crosses. A particularly complex mast has been used for illustration purposes to stress the importance of this procedure. The figure omits one hole that might sometimes be needed. If you intend to hinge the mast then a transverse hole is required about ⅛ in (3 mm) from the foot. In this case, bind the foot of the mast with a few turns of cotton held with nail varnish, to prevent splitting under load. This precaution is not necessary for end-drilled fore-and-aft spars such as booms and gaffs, but in these cases it pays to make the spar a little too long and trim it after the hole has been drilled. Do not forget that terminal holes for stays must be as close to the top of a yard as practical.

As to the practical difficulties of drilling a spar, once it is held in its Blu-Tack bed the most important consideration is to make an accurate centre for the drill. A thin, sharply pointed spike serves this purpose best. One of these is often found in those pocket cases of mixed screwdrivers that can be fitted into a common handle. Since the hole to be drilled will occupy a considerable percentage of the spar's diameter, it goes without saying that the impression made with the spike must be dead centre.

As for the actual drilling, model makers' electric drills are obviously ideal for this work. However, I have used a standard domestic electric drill on many occasions with very little drill bit breakage. It may be found that the drill shank is too small for the chuck in this case. The matter is easily resolved by wrapping a little sticky tape round the shank. You can also obtain modellers' hand-held drill chucks with a short knurled handle, which are twirled between finger and thumb. They are inexpensive, remarkably effective on the soft woods used for bottleships, and unlikely to break the drill bit.

While preparing this book, I met a modeller who prided himself on the extreme delicacy of his work. He used drills as small as one hundredth of an inch so that he could use the most slender of spars. Clearly for so intricate a job the hand-twirled drill (sometimes called a jeweller's drill) is essential. The tiny holes he makes cannot take any ordinary threaded needle; instead, he uses strands of fine nylon thread taken from an old pair of tights and straightened out in hot water or by heating under load, stiffened at the threading end with a blob of glue.

To those readers who wish to produce models of exceptional beauty, this sort of procedure will put you in a very special class of modeller.

The bowsprit and jib-boom

The bowsprit is the spar that projects forward over the vessel's bow and supports the stays that brace the mast and carry the triangular foresails. Larger vessels have heavy bowsprits, usually of square section, overlaid and extended by jib-booms, which support the stays that carry the most forward of the headsails. It is not uncommon for the whole of this assembly to be referred to as the bowsprit.

When the sails are full of wind the upward strain on these spars is considerable and is countered by bracing below the bowsprit with a bobstay. In its simplest form, this consists of a single bracing which extends from the end of the bowsprit to the water-line at the stem. On longer bowsprits the bobstay may be supplemented by bowsprit shrouds which resist side strains on the bowsprit. In large vessels the bowsprit/jib-boom assembly may be stiffened by braces of consider-

able complexity, the strength of which can be substantially increased by straining some of the braces over a spreader which projects from the underside of the bowsprit and is called a dolphin-striker. The model should follow the design of the original as far as practical since the whole assembly adds grace and authenticity to the vessel. Figure 21 shows a variety of these assemblies (without the rigging) and recommended ways of securing the bowsprit to the hull. Even in the model, the bowsprit takes some strain; it should therefore be the first spar to be attached so that the glue has plenty of time to set. Clearly, certain of the fixing holes in the bowsprit can be pre-drilled before the bowsprit is glued to the hull.

Where a dolphin-striker is to be included in the model, it can best be made from a

Figure 21 A variety of bowsprits and their fitting. The holes marked A are best drilled before gluing the bowsprit into place; holes B, through bowsprit and hull, must be drilled after fitting.

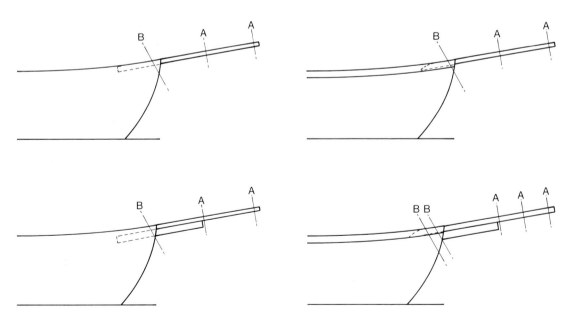

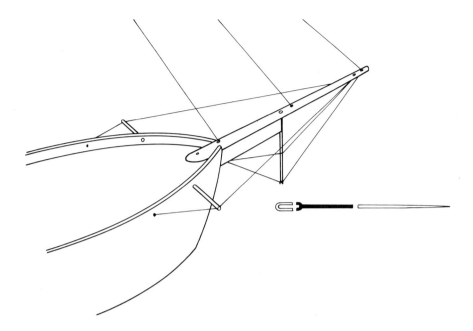

length of fine needle (see figure 22), cut so that a small crutch is left at the bottom as a guide for the threads that will pass under it.

Figure 22 A complex bowsprit assembly, showing also how a dolphin striker can be made from a needle. Because of the problems of sticking and trimming the tightened stays, it is recommended not to attempt more complicated assemblies than this.

The masts

When shaping and cutting the pieces which form the masts, remember these two points. First, the butt of the mast must either be cut cleanly if you are using the hinged method or rounded if the hinge is to be omitted. Second, the top of the mast should be as nicely tapered as the position of the topmost hole permits. Stumpy tops to the masts detract from the appearance of the finished model. The same observation applies to the other spars.

For a first attempt at making one of these models, it would probably be advisable to use the hinge method. Drill a hole through the butt of the mast as close to the foot as possible and form a u-shaped hinge with a thin wire. Very fine ladies' hair pins make good hinge material since they are unobtrusively coloured. Clearly the hinge will operate best if the angles where the wire is bent are sharp, which is nearly impossible to achieve if the bends are made with the wire already through the hole in the mast. The best way is to grip the wire firmly with narrow-nosed pliers and make the bends close to the jaws. Although one tail of the hinge will have to be straightened again to pass through the hole in the mast, it will return reasonably well to its proper shape (see figure 23). Two holes can now be drilled to accept the hinge ends which can, when fitted, be coated with glue.

The second and neater method is to make

a small dimple in the deck where the mast is to be stepped, just large enough to accept the rounded foot of the mast. The dimple can be made with a few twirls of a hand held countersink tool. (Take care not to make it too large.) Obviously, when the mast is collapsed the foot will not remain in the dimple. To ensure that it does not wander too far, a blob of Blu-Tack placed just forward of the mast foot will maintain its approximate position. When the mast has been partly re-erected in the bottle, the mast step can be eased back into the dimple and the Blu-Tack removed (figure 23b) both by use of a wire.

The masts on most larger vessels are made from two or more sections. Where the lower and topmast overlap a small platform called a top is frequently found. Apart from providing a convenient observation or operational location, the top also acts as a spreader for topmast bracing and, though very small, should not be omitted from the model. It can best be made from a scrap of plastic cut from any flat-sided container. Draw the required shape on the plastic scrap, having first taken the gloss off with sandpaper. Now drill a hole for the mast and other holes which when halved will form rigging slots (see figure 24a). The shape can now be cut out and painted – black as a rule – before being glued to the (previously assembled) mast (figures 24b and c). A couple of turns of thread towards the top and bottom of the union, secured with nail varnish, add to the strength and improve the appearance.

Some high masts are made from more than two sections, with a top at the lower junction. Most model spars are out of scale because of the modelling restrictions, so the addition of a third section tends to look clumsy and is better ignored.

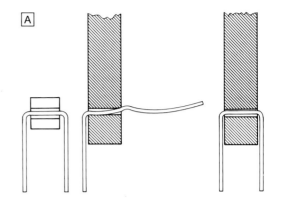

Figure 23 A wire hinge, above, is the traditional way of securing mast to deck, and is easily made from thin wire, shaped first with thin nosed pliers. Blu-Tack and a foothole in the deck, below, make a neater and clever alternative.

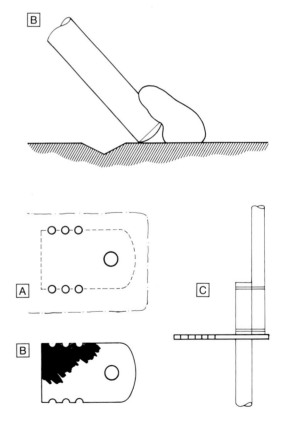

Figure 24 A scrap of plastic can be marked off and drilled to make a top, before being cut out and painted black.

Remaining spars

Few other spars require any special treatment. Yards, booms and gaffs normally have but one hole drilled through them. It is possible, therefore, where relevant, to apply a degree of taper towards their extremities. If done lightly this improves appearances but should not be exaggerated since, in fact, most spars have little or no taper.

Difficult spars

Occasionally vessels carry unusual spars, so positioned that it is impossible to fit them prior to inserting the model into the bottle. Many of the eighteenth-century galleons flew a square sail from a foremast set right out at the end of the bowsprit. Such an assembly obviously cannot be fed through the neck of a bottle in one piece. When building the model, the small platform that is found in such an

assembly at the junction of the bowsprit and the foremast, can be made from two layers of thin plastic sheet. One layer may be glued to the end of the bowsprit, which first needs to be trimmed to produce a horizontal plane. The second may be glued to the bottom of the tiny mast to which the yard and sail can be added. This assembly can now be glued into position after the model has been re-erected inside the bottle. Greater realism is achieved if the yard is under the control of braces, as in all other cases. These can be fitted with plenty of slack before the model is inserted and then drawn up tight, glued and trimmed as a final operation (see figure 25).

Figure 25 The tiny mast and sail on the forward end of a galleon's bowsprit are best fitted when the ship is otherwise complete in the bottle; glue the disc base of the mast B to the disced end of the bowsprit A. When set, adjust the braces and trim off. A careful arrangement of the associated rigging is necessary. Here, all other rigging has been omitted to show the correct fitting of this interesting detail.

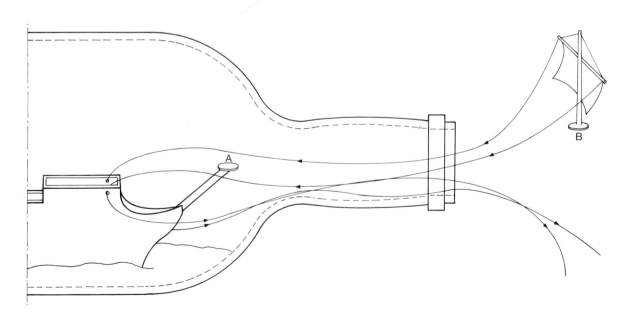

Plate 10   A closer inspection of the brigantine show how
a foaming white sea around the hull strengthens an impression
of movement.

14
Rigging the Model

Before commencing the rigging, the hull must be secured to the build stand and all components painted (see p. 72).

Rigging the bowsprit

From the modeller's point of view bowsprits can be divided into four categories: those without rigging and those with one, two, or four rigging components. The threads should first be tied as close to the extremity of the bowsprit as possible, using the knots shown in figure 26. It will be noted that in all cases only one strand of thread passes over the top of the bowsprit. Arrangements that increase this number detract from the appearance of the model. If there is room and thickness to permit the drilling of a horizontal hole near the tip, then these same knots can be tied through the hole and so avoid any threads over the top of the bowsprit. In this case the bowsprit shroud thread can also pass through this hole and not through the knot.

In the case of the bowsprit with the single thread, an unused tail will be left when the bobstay has been completed. Before cutting off this tail, coat the knot and the tip of the spar with clear nail varnish. When dry, the tail can be cut very close indeed, without any danger of the knot becoming undone. Nail varnish is invaluable for sealing knots thus and as an adhesive for delicate gluing jobs. It dries quickly and leaves no stain or other evidence of its presence.

The thread or threads now secured to the bowsprit must be passed, using a fine needle, through the holes drilled in the hull to receive them. If the holes are over $\frac{3}{16}$ in (4.5 mm) long, and the last bit of thread to be pulled through the hole is coated with varnish, the tail can be cut off as soon as the varnish is dry. Where the threads pass through the thinner bulkheads or bulwarks, the same procedure can be adopted, but a $\frac{1}{4}$ in (6 mm) tail should be left to brush into the angle between the bulwark and the deck, with a little more varnish (see figure 27).

On some of the larger vessels, the arrangement of rigging around the bowsprit becomes extremely complex and in such cases you would do well to formalize the layout, so that no more than four threads are used. Otherwise the model begins to look clumsy and with an over-complex arrangement of threads in this zone it becomes increasingly difficult to cut off the ends of the stays after re-erection in the bottle, without damaging other threads.

Rigging the shrouds

Hold the mast upright on its hinge or over its dimple with a blob of the ubiquitous Blu-Tack and check that the holes drilled through the bulwarks are all just aft of the mast and correspond with the design from which you are working. As pointed out earlier, not all vessels have convenient bulkheads through which to thread the shrouds (see pp. 50–51).

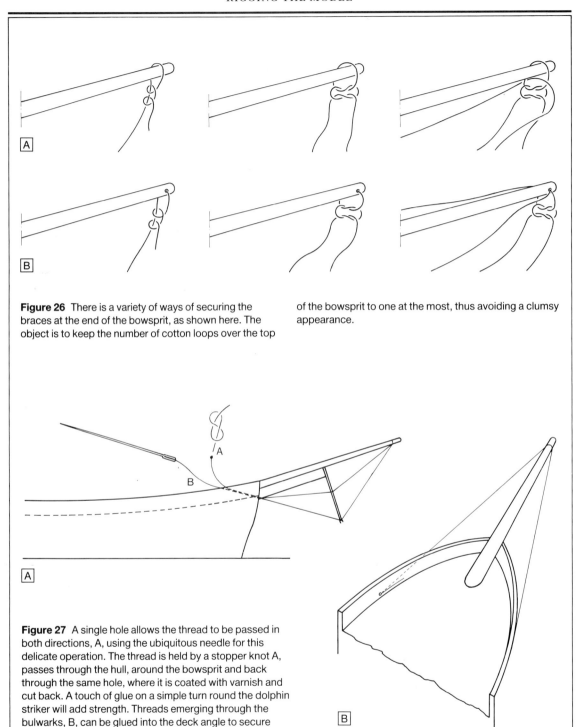

Figure 26 There is a variety of ways of securing the braces at the end of the bowsprit, as shown here. The object is to keep the number of cotton loops over the top of the bowsprit to one at the most, thus avoiding a clumsy appearance.

Figure 27 A single hole allows the thread to be passed in both directions, A, using the ubiquitous needle for this delicate operation. The thread is held by a stopper knot A, passes through the hull, around the bowsprit and back through the same hole, where it is coated with varnish and cut back. A touch of glue on a simple turn round the dolphin striker will add strength. Threads emerging through the bulwarks, B, can be glued into the deck angle to secure them.

Now thread a fine needle and tie a stopper knot, such as the figure of eight knot shown in figure 28a, at the end of the thread. The figure illustrates a simple arrangement but precisely the same procedure is adopted for the more complex shroud arrangements shown in figure 28b. Five shrouds are about the most that can be accommodated along the average model's gunwale, no matter how many are present on the full-sized vessel and, despite what is shown in figure 28b, they would normally pass through more than one hole in the mast.

Figure 28 A single length of thread is used to build up either a simple, A, or a complex, B, system of shrouds, keeping the number of stopper knots or glued tails to an absolute minimum.

When you start to thread the shrouds, first check that the stopper knot is a tight fit in the first hole. If not tie it afresh on the bight to produce a bulkier knot. Draw the knot, coated with nail varnish, just inside the hole.

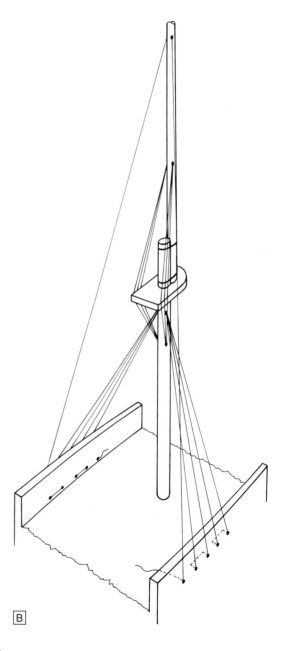

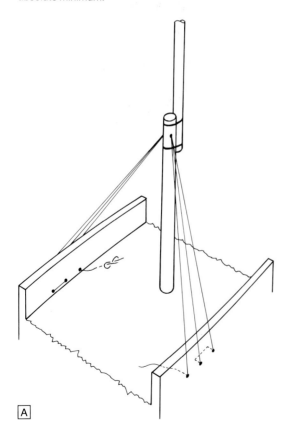

A

B

The tail can be cut off close to the hull when the varnish has hardened. Having completed the threading and tensioning, finish off by backstitching through the previous hole and securing the thread along the inside of the bulwark with varnish. Cut off the surplus thread when the nail varnish has hardened. Before you seal off in this way, support the top of the mast with a finger, ensuring that it is either upright or heeled aft, according to your design. Now adjust the tension in all shrouds so that each is equally tight and the mast will not be pulled forward by the stays, which are the next items of rigging to be fitted. Finally, apply a spot of nail varnish to each of the shroud holes through the mast to maintain stability in all planes.

Some ships are flush-decked, i.e. have guard-rails rather than solid bulwarks. Since guard-rails are impossibly fiddly to repro-duce on a small-scale model, other methods of threading the shrouds must be adopted.

Without a jig, it is not practical to drill straight through the hull with any prospect of the emerging holes being in any sort of acceptable alignment. If there are few masts and shrouds, holes can be drilled diagonally

from both sides, emerging somewhere near the water-line (see figure 29). The shrouds can then be threaded much as before. Cover the stitches with a touch of the hull paint and, if they are close enough to the water-line they should be hard to detect. In most cases it will be neater to make tiny eyelets from the very fine wire used in most electric flexes. Loop a small hairpin of the wire over a needle which is a trifle larger than the one used for threading and twist it to form an eye

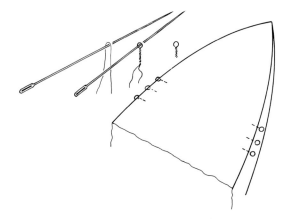

Figure 30 Another way of dealing with shrouds without bulwarks; small eyes made from twisted wire are glued into the hull to receive the shrouds.

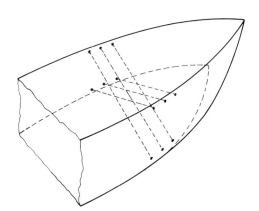

Figure 29 Vessels without gunwales, or bulwarks, can take their shrouds into holes drilled through the hull and down to the opposite waterline.

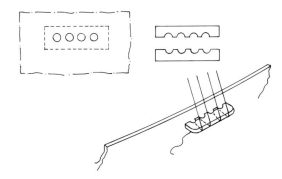

Figure 31 Shroud plates found on some older galleons make a prominent feature of the shroud anchorages, shown here drilled, then cut, then in use.

with a wound tail. Cut to about ³/₁₆ in (4.5 mm) long and glue into holes which have been drilled part way through the hull from both sides. Ensure that all the eyes lie in the vertical plane (see figure 30).

Some galleons will be seen to have shroud plates. They project from the ship's sides and form quite a distinctive feature of this type of craft. Where this occurs, the plates can be marked out on a piece of plastic in much the same way as the mast tops illustrated in figures 24a-c. Cut them out as narrowly as possible to avoid a clumsy-looking feature and to reduce the leverage and consequent strain on the narrow glued surface when the shrouds are tightened (see figure 31).

Rigging the stays

The stays are the most vital items of rigging. They control the raising and lowering of the masts as well as sharing with the shrouds the job of maintaining the masts rigidly upright. All masts will have one or more of them, and all will pass through running-holes in the bowsprit, or through the mast or masts further forward, or through the deck to emerge near the water-line. All will have long tails initially. The tidiest way of attaching the stays to the mast is by jamming a stopper knot into a hole in the mast in much the same way as that used for starting the threading of the shrouds. Where this is not practical

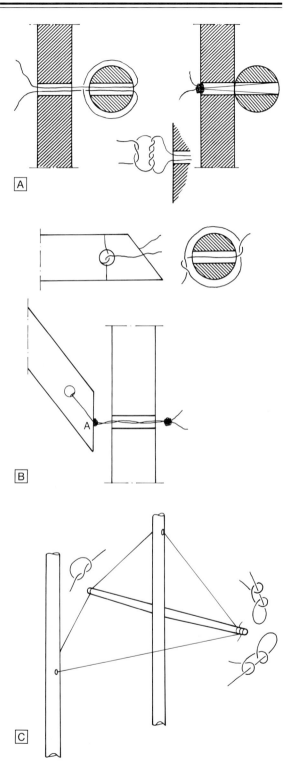

Figure 32 (*right*) Yards are secured to the mast by a single thread, as in A. The fixing should not be too tight, since the yard must be rotated to lie alongside the mast when entering the bottle. The detail shows how to tie the stopper knot, which can be touched with varnish when drawn into the hole. Gaff and boom, B, are similarly fixed, again with sufficient mobility to allow them to hinge upwards. Yard rigging is secured as in C, locking each knot with a touch of varnish.

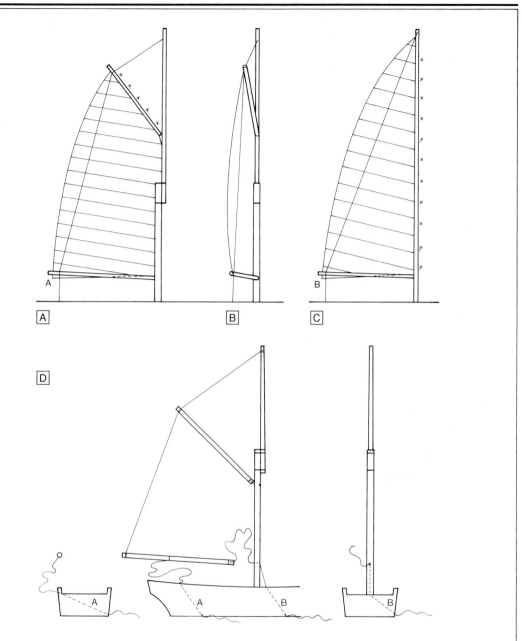

Figure 33 A simple way of rigging the fore and aft sails, A. Cut the clew a little low to give belly to the sail when lifted to the boom top, and glue the sail only to the gaff, marked X, or to the mast where there's no gaff. Tie threads to the right side of the boom, as shown in the centre, to make a step for the foot of the sail. The only disadvantage of this method is the slightly awkward task of lifting the foot of the sail on to the boom after the ship has been otherwise reconstructed within its bottle. A more complicated alternative is shown in D, below, where the sail is attached to both gaff and boom and sets itself in the bottle when all lines have been tightened. Draw threads A and B tight when fixing the sail, but introduce slack as shown when collapsing the spars.

because of the close proximity of other holes, your design will show that it has to be tied. Use the half round turn and two half hitches illustrated in figure 26. During this operation the masts can be held in position with a ring of Blu-Tack round the foot. Whichever method you use, do not be impatient. The sealing varnish must be fully hardened before trimming and the stay should be given a gentle tug to check its security. A stay which parts from the mast during erection in the bottle does not bear contemplation. After threading the stays through the appropriate hole or holes, make the tails fast to the cleats on the side of the build stand so that there is reasonable tension in both the shrouds and stays. The Blu-Tack that has helped support the masts so far can now be removed.

Fitting the remaining spars to the masts

The essential requirement of all other spars is that they can be laid close alongside their parent masts to form part of the vital 'sausage' at the time of insertion. Therefore yards must rotate and fore-and-aft spars must hinge (see figure 32). As explained in the design section, there is little to be gained aesthetically by including foresail sheets in the rigging programme. In life these ropes are kept under tension by the pressure of the wind in the sails they control; on a model they droop untidily.

The need to rig the fore-and-aft sails rigidly, with a thread which is tied from mast head to gaff, to boom and so to the port-side gunwale has already been mentioned. The arrangement shown in figure 12 for an independent sheet A can often be combined with the general rigging of these spars, as illustrated in figure 33. In this case, the thread should be knotted on the starboard side of the boom to provide a step for the foot of the sail.

However, there is an alternative layout, shown in figure 33d, the possible advantages of which will also be considered when discussing sail fitting.

We have now dealt with all the main spars associated with the masts, but not with the minor spars which are part of the bowsprit assembly, as described earlier. Since they play no part in the erection of the masts or the setting of the sails, these bowsprit spars can be fitted at any time when there is a pause in the tensioning of the stays while the nail-varnished stopper knots or ties are drying out. If the bowsprit rigging is at all complex, as it may well be, study closely the proximity of these static lines to the loose tails of those stays which require tightening and final gluing and trimming after the ship is inside the bottle. You have to decide, before the ship goes into its bottle, how you are going to execute this gluing and trimming. Whatever you use as a trimming instrument, most probably a surgeon's scalpel, must not only be exceedingly sharp, but because you will be working within a confined area, with limited manoeuvrability, it may also be necessary to mask all but the very shortest length of exposed blade to reduce the risk of cutting a bowsprit shroud by accident.

Plate 11   An unfamiliar starboard quarter view of the
Cutty Sark under full canvas: see page 88.

15
Making the Sails

Square sails

Although many of the old models are canvassed with sails made from the finest cloth available aboard, they still appear coarse on a small model. They are also difficult to arrange in the pleasing curves which wind-filled sails exhibit. Their main advantage lies in the ease with which they can be bundled for insertion in the bottle. They also resist creasing during this process.

Greater realism can be achieved with very fine paper. The most suitable is the flimsy paper used by typists for multiple copies. First remove the glaring whiteness by soaking the paper for some hours, preferably overnight, in a tray of tea or coffee, which will turn it, when dry, to a more natural hue. It will probably be cockled and will require ironing.

There are several variations of method in sail manufacture. The simplest is to produce a 'sail cloth', by drawing parallel lines over a sufficient area of the paper, at about $\frac{1}{8}$ in (3 mm) intervals, with a well-sharpened chisel-edged pencil. Repeat on the reverse side of the paper, endeavouring to follow the course of the lines on the first side. Now trace off, or copy the sail layout from the work drawing. If the intention is to produce a model of an old vessel which has been long at sea, repair patches can be added to the sails, with a few touches of a watercolour paint that varies only slightly from the background colour of the paper (see figure 14, p. 38). When cutting out the square sails, leave a $\frac{1}{4}$ in (6 mm) tab beyond the head of the sail. Fold the tab over towards what will be the back of the sail to produce a sharp crease along the head and trim it, leaving about $\frac{1}{32}$ in (0.5 mm) to stick to the underside of the yard. Use nail varnish for this and assist adhesion by pinching with some fine-nosed tweezers. At the same time try to roll some curvature into the sail.

A modification of this method is to cut out two copies of each sail and paste them, unlined sides together, rolled around a piece of broom handle or heavy dowel. Remove them before they are fully dry otherwise they may well stick to the wood. Allow them to finish drying in the curved shape. Being thicker, they will tend to retain this shape during subsequent handling though they are a little more difficult to roll neatly when they go into the sausage. I recommend, therefore, that when first trying this or the following method you should be making a vessel with few square sails.

The third method is much the same as the second, but in this case the whole length of the broom handle is covered with a piece of 'sail cloth' (single-sided, lines down), secured with drawing pins or sticky tape to form a firm tube. Paste the cut-out sails, lines up, to this tube and leave to dry. With both double-skinned methods leave the sails a little oversized for final trimming.

69

Fore-and-aft sails other than staysails

The same general method can be employed as with square sails. However, there is little to be gained by making them double-skinned. They are harder to keep in good shape after 'sausaging' but, fortunately, any irregularities in the setting are less significant than with square or staysails. They must be cut very carefully indeed to fit precisely into the exact area bounded by the mast, boom and gaff. If the simple layout of spars is used, the sail can be glued to the gaff only. If any other attachment is made, you will not be able to fold the boom and gaff into their sausage shape without tearing the sail. Once the ship is in the bottle you will need to manipulate the sail into its snug position with a length of bent wire. To assist with this, cut the foot of the sail to precisely the right length at the luff (the edge near the mast) but make it a trifle overlong at the leech (the after edge; see figure 33). After erection in the bottle, this corner of the sail (the clew) can be lifted onto the top of the boom with the wire. The pressure exerted when the sail is positioned thus will hold it firm and also put a little curvature into it. As an extra precaution it is possible, with care, to apply a spot of nail varnish to this corner from the wire to lessen the chance of the sail coming out again when you adjust the rest of the rigging. This is one of the most exacting of the manoeuvres met in this rewarding pursuit. But if your early attempts do not prove entirely satisfactory, at least any faults will be less obvious than with, say, badly set square sails.

If, however, the alternative for fitting the boom is used (see figure 33d) the sail can be glued to both the gaff and the boom. This method is particularly useful when dealing with a fore-and-aft sail which is caged in several items of rigging, including possibly the braces from the square sails on the more forward mast, making manipulations with a bent wire somewhat tedious. The disadvantage lies in the extra threads needed, which emerge from the hull where there is likely to be a certain amount of glue when the vessel is being fixed inside the bottle. Clearly, these threads must not be allowed to stick before they have been drawn.

Furthermore, if the Blu-Tack method of controlling the mast foot is used, there must be adequate free thread between the mast and the boom end, since the Blu-Tack will, until flicked off, inhibit the movement of this thread.

In the case of triangular Bermuda sails, where there is no gaff, the luff can be glued directly to the mast (also shown in figure 33). This makes the task much easier, but unfortunately, whilst the Bermuda sail is almost universal on modern boats, it does not appear on the older square-riggers that the modeller is likely to favour.

Staysails

Very occasionally these sails are fitted with a jib-boom, a light spar that supports the foot of the sail. The vast majority are loose-footed, supported only by the stay from which they are set. The best method of attachment, therefore, is to fold double-sided sails around the stays and paste the two halves together. Draw the sail and its image on the prepared paper and pencil in the seams (see figure 34 for alternative seam markings).

Before attaching the sail, snip off the cor-

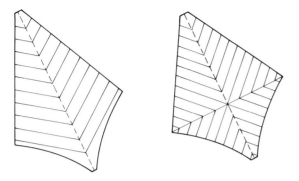

Figure 34 The headsail before being folded and glued together round its stay. Note the alternative patterns of the seams.

Furled sails

In strong winds some of the lower sails are furled to ease the strain on the gear. In action, warships usually furl all the lower sails, called courses, to reduce fire hazard, and to improve all-round visibility. This effect can be achieved by following the instructions accompanying figure 35. (Do not forget to stain the tissue paper used for these sails before use.)

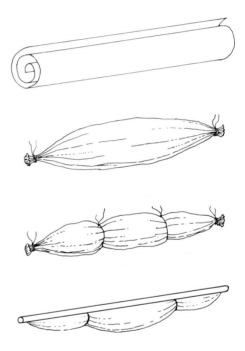

Figure 35 To make furled sails, first roll up the sail, then tie up both ends tightly and work the resulting bundle with your fingers to achieve the crumpled effect of canvas rolled or folded on itself. Loop two threads around the bundle as shown, tying them loosely, then push one edge of the bundle flat and glue it beneath the supporting yard, trimming surplus material as necessary. Nail varnish on the two spacer threads will keep the furled sail in the required shape.

ners at each end of the fold, otherwise little points will stand away from the stay. Work a curvature into the sail with finger and thumb whilst it is being set round the stay so that it is filling on the port side of the vessel. I have suggested (p. 25) that the vessel should be on starboard tack, i.e. with the wind blowing from the starboard side, and can now reveal why. Because of the way in which cotton is laid up there is a tendency for it to twist in an anti-clockwise direction when put under tension. Thus when the stays are finally tightened any sails attached to them will also rotate marginally in that direction, which will imply a starboard tack.

Some staysails must be left free to slide on the stay. Where a stay passes through a hole on the next mast aft and terminates at the following one, the stay must be free to slide along the fold in the sail. Take care, therefore, to keep the fold and the stay clean of paste. It will be found that there is quite sufficient friction in the fold for the sail to hold the position into which it is finally adjusted.

16
Painting and Embellishing

The hull

The hull should be painted on the build stand after you have completed drilling. To keep the stand clean a piece of, say, grease-proof paper should be sandwiched between hull and stand top.

The hulls of many historical ships were painted black, which from the modeller's point of view is a pity. However, if a type rather than a specific vessel is being modelled, then some choice can be allowed. Colours, even so, should be muted. The decks and the inside of the bulwarks should be stained light oak or a similar colour.

Galleons and other older ships, however, were frequently painted in the gayest colours. If you are designing one from a black and white drawing, look at coloured pictures of similar vessels to form an idea of the likely colours.

Do not attempt to add further decoration with paint, unless the area affected is relatively large. White or gold lines, which occur frequently, can best be reproduced with threads of cotton, fixed with our old friend colourless nail varnish. In the same way, decorative swirls, usually gold, can be represented by covering the small area with varnish and working a design of yellow cotton into it with the point of a needle. White squares or gun ports can be cut from paper, and these too can be stuck to the sides of the hull. Once the ship is in the bottle, it is extremely difficult to spot that the decorations have been applied in this way.

The spars

After shaping and drilling, the spars should be treated with a light oak stain unless your pattern indicates something quite different. They should not normally be varnished. Tops (see p. 58) are usually black, and should be painted before fixing to the mast. Sometimes the lower masts and sometimes also the mast tips and the extremities of other spars are painted white. This touching in of the yard ends and mast tips gives a pleasing appearance, but should not be done until the vessel is complete in all other respects, so that the pristine whiteness is not dulled by handling. Use the paint sparingly.

The sails

Suggestions for seaming and patching are given on p. 69. Many ancient vessels had considerable ornamentation on their sails. In some cases this can be reproduced using coloured paper, but if the design is too small for this treatment, and since the most popular colours are red and blue, you can successfully apply it with a standard ball-point pen. The same goes for black symbols and numbers on a modern sail.

Rigging

I prefer black cotton for all rigging. Some people prefer dark brown, whilst others favour black for the standing rigging, in real life normally made of wire, and brown for the running rigging, which is usually rope. Shrouds are tensioned with blocks and tackle at their lower ends. The vessel's appearance is improved if a minute spot of white paint is applied to each shroud about an eighth of an inch above the bulwarks, but dots must be small, even and regular or the effect is spoilt.

Flags

Flags fall into four main categories:
1 The Union flag, only called the Union Jack when flown from a jack-staff. It is hoisted in the bow of the vessel or, on some old men-of-war, half way out on the bow-sprit. It may only be flown on ships of the Royal Navy.
2 The colours, or national ensign. In the case of Great Britain we have three ensigns and variations of them: the white ensign, introduced in 1803, flown right aft by the Royal Navy or Royal Yacht Squadron; the blue ensign, flown as a privilege by members of certain clubs associated with the navy; the red ensign, which should be flown by all other British vessels and by ships of the Royal Navy prior to 1803. It is always flown on a staff aft or from the nearest point in the rigging.
3 House or club flags of individual design, which are flown from the mast head.
4 Signal flags, which are flown singly or in groups from crosstrees or other visible and convenient points, as required.

Draw the shape of the flag on a suitable piece of paper, leaving room for a mirror image of the flag to fly in reverse from its leading edge. Colour the flag, following as carefully as possible your chosen design, and take the colour over the three outside edges. Now fold the paper along the line of the leading edge of the flag, and cut out the flag's shape through the two sheets of paper. Colour the other side of your flag, again taking the colour over the now cut edges. The two sides of the flag are glued together only when the flag is put into its final position on the model.

Plate 12   Putting a complicated model like the author's clipper into a bottle calls for care, patience and a delicate touch: but the effect is worth all the effort. See pages 68 and 88.

17
Fitting the Ship into the Bottle

And so to the moment of truth! Check that the sea in the bottle is very firm, and preferably completely dried out. Check that the base upon which the ship will be glued is well set in the putty. Supposing, by some unlikely and unlucky chance, the base is discovered to be loose: remove it, apply generous glue to both surfaces, replace and leave it for a day to ensure its security. Now make one last check on the available height in the bottle. This is the last chance to make any adjustments.

The model can now be removed from the workstand. If the masts have not been hinged, then a small blob of Blu-Tack must be set forward of each mast foot to discourage it from sliding too far forward for easy re-erection.

Collapse the masts with care. Ensure that shrouds and other items of rigging which now become slack, lie tidily between the masts, or in whatever their correct relationship with other parts of the vessel might be. This check may well save a critical situation during re-erection, when odd items of rigging are found to be wrapped round some projection. (There is a law which ordains that this will inevitably be the one which is the most difficult to unscramble!)

When the rigging is partly collapsed, so that the tension has gone off the braces, rotate the yards to lie alongside the masts. Make rolls of the square sails, creasing them as little as possible. The mast, yard and square sail assembly should be as pencil-like as practical. Now make a fairly loose roll of the fore-and-aft sails. Because each of these will simply be glued to its gaff and will be like an awkward flag, it needs to be carefully arranged. Time spent in achieving the neatest possible sausage will be saved later, when smoothing out irregularities after erection. Now apply a coat of general-purpose (not impact) glue to the sea base and the underside of the hull with the same bent oil brush that was used to paint the wave tops.

Then, humming a sea shanty through clenched teeth, slide the sausage through the neck of the bottle. You see, it takes only a few words to say it. Make sure of course, that all the long stay tails are left hanging out of the neck. Manoeuvre the hull onto the sea bed with a pair of surgeon's forceps (if you are lucky enough to be able to obtain so useful a tool) or use tongs you have made yourself from about 20 in (50 cms) of coat-hanger wire, the ends rolled over to produce a gripping area. Press down on as many parts of the deck or bulwarks as can be reached to assist the bond between the hull and its base. The aftermast will probably have lifted slightly already from its contact with the bottom of the bottle. Other masts can be eased forward a little so that a check can be made that all the rigging is free and not trapped under the hull, or otherwise in trouble. The stays, which by now will be in a twisted state, can be tidied up and stuck around the outside of the bottle with blobs of Blu-Tack to ensure that they remain untangled. And this is all you can do until the glue under the hull has set. Don't be impatient to proceed further. If a particularly complex arrangement of stays has been employed (they can approach double figures in some cases), the waiting time might well be spent in tracking each one by eye, and adding an identifying label to its tail. You will find that when tensioning commences practically everything moves, no matter which stay is pulled, and an orderly erection becomes more difficult.

When the glue has set sufficiently to hold the model securely, try to raise the masts, working in order from the front. If other masts begin to lift, it may be because stays which pass through the foremast are holding by friction, which does not matter. On the other hand, it may be because of a caught shroud, which should be released before damage is caused. As each mast rises to about three-quarters of the way up, pause and edge the mast step back into its dimple before completing the lift, using the same probe to flick out the Blu-Tack.

Now fully tension each stay in turn. Starting with the foremost stay, hold the tail so that the thread lies along the underside of the bowsprit, and stroke the point of contact with the bent brush charged with glue. Maintain the tension until it is holding well. Continue in the same way with all the stays, sticking those that pass through the hull as close to the water line as possible. When all is dry, cut off the tails as close as possible to the point of contact. The ideal tool for this purpose is a surgeon's scalpel. Failing this, any small blade secured to a long handle must suffice. In either case, cover most of the blade with some adhesive tape so that only the extreme tip is exposed for cutting. This will ensure that no other threads in the vicinity are severed by accident.

Any fluffy ends left after cutting can be smoothed away with a touch of nail varnish. With a wire probe, the angles and set of the sails can now be adjusted, working forward from the aftermost mast. This will include the delicate job of setting the mizen sail on its boom (see page 66). As shown in figure 33, a more complicated way of setting up the boom to carry a fore and aft sail can be adopted. It may not be entirely clear that the purpose of this arrangement is to allow the sail to be secured to both the boom and the gaff, rather than to the gaff alone as in the simpler set up. Because the boom is entirely free when the control lines are slack, there is no difficulty in combining the boom, the gaff and the sail into a single slim bundle, as part of the entry 'sausage'. This arrangement is of particular value when it is difficult to reach the sail with a probe in order to lift its foot onto the boom. In this case, the mere tightening of the control lines automatically sets the sail correctly. Jibs and other stay sails should be eased out into their natural positions, though those glued to the stays have probably swung to port already.

It may be found that, despite all your care to give the sails the easiest passage possible through the bottle neck, some unacceptably obvious creases have formed. Shape a wire probe to reach the back of the creased sail and attach to its end a small ball of cotton wool soaked in water. Gently stroke the sail until the crease has been reduced to acceptable proportions or has vanished entirely.

At this stage or earlier, take the ubiquitous wire probe and shape it to reach the positions of such items as deck houses, lifeboats (other than those already positioned over the stern), smoke stacks etc., which were too large to become part of the sausage. Stick these items, appropriately glued, one by one to the probe with a blob of Blu-Tack (how valuable this material is proving), and edge them into their approximate positions. Wriggle the probe to detach the Blu Tack and hook it out. Now adjust the position of the added component with the probe, while the glue is still tacky.

I have not bothered to discuss the way in which these embellishments can be made and whether or not they can be added before entry or afterwards, since this is well within any modeller's scope and not a central design problem. It might, however, help if the manufacture of ships' boats is considered. The carving is most easily accomplished by first preparing a square sectioned stick of the appropriate size (⅛ in (3 mm) square will usually serve). The stick can be held in a vice or under the clamp whilst the end is shaped, finishing at the stern cut off. For a boat that is to be positioned keel up on the deck, concentrate on the underside and leave the top flat for easy gluing. For a boat to be hung on davits, the keel becomes less important but the top should be slightly curved fore and aft to produce sheer, and so add realism. The model is too small to attempt any further detail. (See figure 36 for the fitting of the davits.) Those that hang over the ship's side, and therefore have to be added after the ship is bottled, carry the davits with them. The fixing contact is between the boat and the side of the vessel and the davits simply rest on the deck.

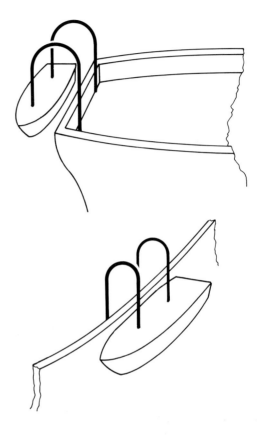

Figure 36 The ship's boat can be hung from davits over the stern, A, an arrangement common to brigantines and similar vessels. The davits are glued inside the stern gunwale, and positioned before the ship enters the bottle. If the boat hangs over the ship's side, it can only be positioned after the model has been re-erected in the bottle. In this case the boat itself must be glued direct to the ship's side. See also figure 15C.

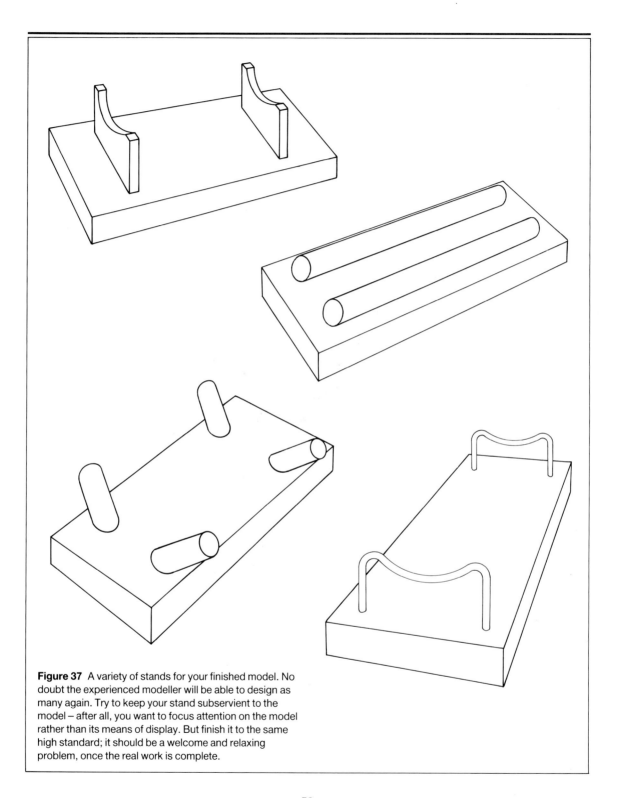

Figure 37 A variety of stands for your finished model. No doubt the experienced modeller will be able to design as many again. Try to keep your stand subservient to the model – after all, you want to focus attention on the model rather than its means of display. But finish it to the same high standard; it should be a welcome and relaxing problem, once the real work is complete.

18
Final Touches

Your work is now virtually complete, except for presentation. Leave the bottle uncorked and on top of a radiator or other warm spot for a minimum of a week. It is amazing how long complete drying takes from this enclosed space. Even when thoroughly dried, the model should never be displayed in direct sunlight. A mist might well form inside the glass and will not disperse until the bottle has cooled again.

When satisfied, drive a cork into the neck and slice off any excess beyond the top. Now add a coating of sealing wax over the cork top. This is best dripped on from one of those sticks which incorporates its own wick.

Now if you do not know how to tie a Turk's head (that plaited collar of decorative string which sets off the neck of the bottle) ask a sailing friend to help you. In my experience, this is one of the more difficult knots to learn

from a diagram! 2 mm or 3 mm plaited nylon or Terylene cord is the best material for the collar.

If the bottle does not stand conveniently without support then it will be necessary to make a stand for it. Several examples are shown in figure 37.

For special models it is worth having a plate etched for fixing to the display stand, giving the name of the vessel, the modeller's name and the date.

Finally, make sure that the outside of your bottle is kept clean and sparkling. Constant handling during the modelling process can make it surprisingly mucky. So before it goes on display, give it a thorough, but very careful, surface wash with a liquid detergent, dry it off at once, and polish it. Try to keep your model immaculate. It has, after all, taken you many hours to assemble.

Part III

PROJECTS

Now you have mastered both the design process and the techniques of modelling, you are ready to begin your first complete project. There are five designs in the following pages to set you on the way. Start with the simpler models, and you will soon discover that the more complicated vessels are just as easy to build – but take a lot more time and patience. Take each step as it comes, and complete it, before you tackle the next one, and with every model you build try to improve on what you have already achieved.

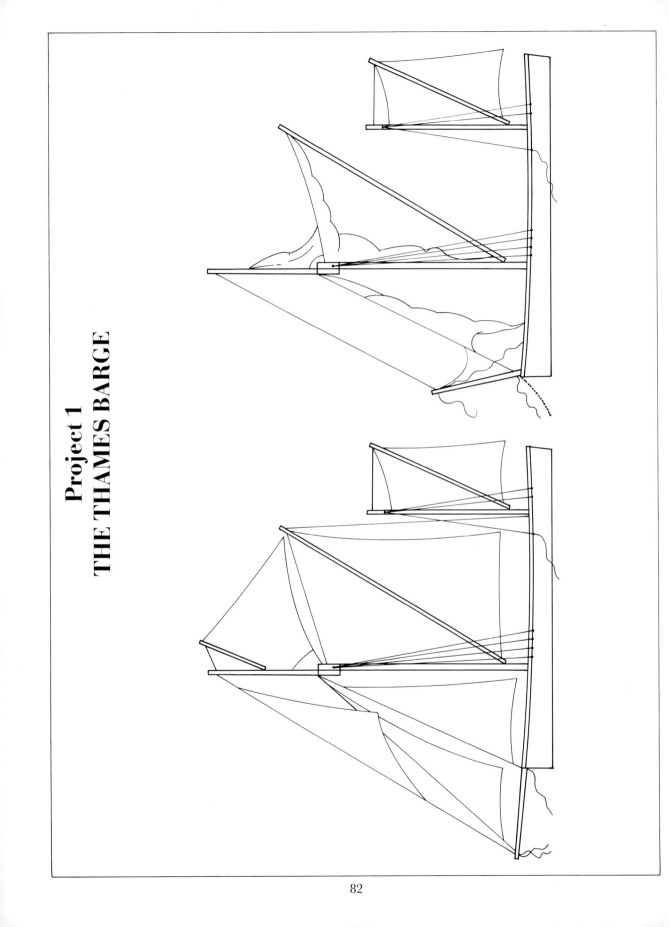

Project 1
THE THAMES BARGE

Not so very long ago there were many examples of this fine old workhorse to be seen on the Thames, when it was still a commercial waterway. Easily identified by its dark reddish-brown sails, the Thames barge is straight stemmed and square sterned, has only two masts, loose-footed sails ketch-rigged as shown here, no booms, and only three diagonal spars, which can be easily folded up against the masts for entry into the bottle. The distance between the masts allows for a large hatch amidships; these barges carried every kind of cargo. A smaller hatch is forward of the main mast, and at the stern a low entry leads to the cabin below the quarter deck. The hull is painted black, with a white upper edge.

One barge is shown under full sail, the second with its sails largely furled. Both can be put into a single bottle, if suitably sealed, on a calm water, the one moored to a colourful buoy, the other complete with bow wave and white wake. To make your models, proceed as follows:

1 Carve the hull, complete with bulwarks, as described on page 45. If this is your first model, take great care not to cut away too much of the hull block at one time, and try to keep the bulwarks just thick enough not to split, without being too obviously out of scale.

2 Make the spars, as described on page 53. Even with simple spars and masts such as these, you are advised to make a drilling chart. Without one, it is all too easy to miss a hole during the drilling programme, which proves extremely awkward later on. A wire mast hinge is easier to manage at this stage – you can experiment with the Blu-Tack method when you have more experience. The bowsprit is hinged in operational barges, as you see from the moored example, but there is no need to hinge your model.

3 The rigging is straightforward, apart from the pair of stays supporting the mizen mast, which pass through the bulwarks on either side. Sticking and trimming is a little more difficult when the tails emerge near the stern of the vessel. However, there are no bowsprit shrouds, which simplifies the securing of the forward stays.

4 The sails are easy to make, but should be stained to a suitable russet colour with water paint, rather than the usual light tea or coffee staining. The foremost staysail set high may be left white, to contrast with the other sails, but on a working vessel it would almost certainly have looked a very dirty grey.

5 Complete the model by adding deck details and embellishments. Some barges carried their lifebelts secured to the mizen mast stays, head height above the deck: this makes an interesting feature. When your model is complete in the bottle, check the set of the single line which supports the diagonal spar on the mizen. If it is not reasonably straight, coat it with nail varnish and push it backwards with a probe for a minute or two until it sets, so it looks as though it is properly under tension.

Project 2
THE BRIXHAM TRAWLER

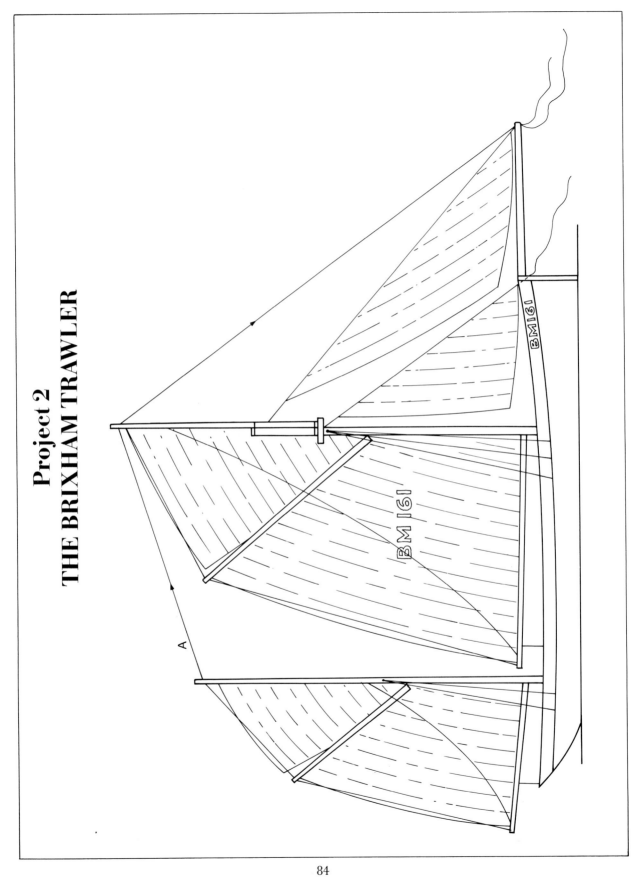

This is a similar vessel to the Thames barge, a slow, heavy, strongly built sea going craft, a good all-weather boat, once familiar in fishing ports all round British coasts, but long since replaced by tubby steel trawlers. Even those are much reduced in number, with the decline in the fishing industry, but of the Brixham trawler hardly a single example survives. The hull has a strong straight stem, an elegant counter stern and high bulwarks, which can be painted to contrast the usually black hull. In the drawing above, the stay A between the masts and down to the end of the boom at the foot of the lower spanker (the rearmost sail) is modeller's licence: not on the working vessel, this extra stay is needed to raise the after mast in the bottle. Making the model proceeds as for the Thames barge:

1 Carve the hull and bulwarks. Cut back the stern underneath the quarter deck as far as you can, to reproduce that handsome counter.

2 Making the spars is quite straightforward, as previously described. The foremast on this and the Thames barge is in two sections, but on the Brixham trawler the joining of the masts is completed by a top (see figure 24). The hole drilled in the top should be big enough to accommodate both the overlapping mast sections, making a tight fit. The joining surfaces of the masts should be slightly flattened with a file to provide a good gluing surface. A neat tie around each end of the overlap, one immediately above the top and the higher above that, around the end of the lower mast, will look neat and add extra security. Seal the ties with a dab of glue or nail varnish.

3 The rigging should present few problems, but because you now have to deal with two sizeable booms, you should decide which method of rigging to choose (see figure 33). I prefer to cut the clews a little low, and then lift the sails on to their booms with a probe, once the ship is in the bottle. In this way, the sail takes up a slight curve, pleasing to look at, and kept in place by the 'spring' in the extra material. The associated rigging must pass on the opposite side of the boom to provide a resting place for the lifted end of the sail; at this point, a dab of glue can be neatly applied by probe through the neck of the bottle.

4 When you make the sails, don't forget to soak the paper in tea or coffee overnight to reduce the brilliance of the original finish. Line in the panel seams, and draw the vessel's identification number – here it is BM 161, BM being the first and last letter of the port of registration, a system still used today – on the main sail or the lower spanker. The same number should be painted on the bows and across the stern. If you prefer the russet sails of the Thames barge, try the same colour for your Brixham trawler; many working boats would have sported this colour.

5 Add whatever deck fittings you have room for, remembering that the original would have been fairly basic. This was a vessel on and from which hardened old salts earned a tough and often dangerous living.

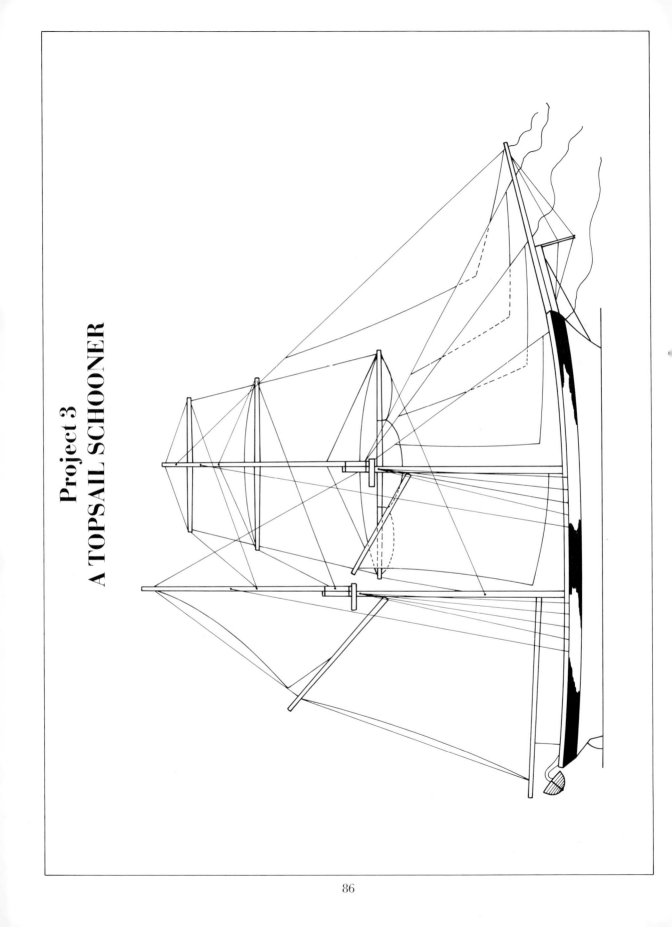

Project 3
A TOPSAIL SCHOONER

The schooner was a widely used deep sea light cargo ship of the last century, surviving well into the age of the steamship; there were still many examples working commercially in the 1920s and 30s, and the last schooners were built as late as the 1920s. Like the example shown here, a schooner is typically a two-masted ship, with both the fore and main sails rigged fore and aft, but many American schooners carried three, four, five or six masts. One was built with seven (a fearsome ship to model in a bottle, if you ever find a drawing of the *Thomas W. Lawson*). The longest wooden ship ever built was the six masted schooner *Wyoming*, 1909, all of 330 feet from stem to stern. Topsails on smaller schooners like ours can be square rigged, as here, or fore and aft. A double topsail schooner also carries two square sails on the main mast, which is not much higher than the foremast and usually positioned near midship. A brigantine is very much like a schooner, but has three rather than two square sails on the foremast, the third taking the place of the fourth staysail carried by the topsail schooner, and the more complex brig carries three square sails on the main mast as well. From all of this it follows that, with some ingenuity, you can devise at least four different ships from this one drawing.

Modelling the schooner presents no new problems, apart from an evidently increasing complexity. Proceed in the usual order:

1 Begin with the hull, which as with our earlier models is bulwarked all round.

2 Make the spars according to previous instructions, but note that this time there are yards for the square sails. Spars become more numerous as the projects become more advanced, so in order to avoid confusion (it can take a lot of sorting out if you keep all your spars in a heap) it is a good idea to cut and drill it, to the working plan with a small touch of Blu-Tack. There are two masts, both of two sections, to be joined with tops as before. Keep your drill plan for each mast clearly labelled.

3 It may look a complicated rigging plan, but proceed according to earlier instructions and it will all work when you come to bottle your schooner. The bowsprit carries a dolphin striker and associated rigging, but there are no bowsprit shrouds to complicate things any further. When you come to erect the model, raise the masts half way only and check that all rigging is running free before completing the erection.

4 However complicated your model, and however many sails it carries, making the sails is always the same straightforward process. The schooner is a handsome ship and deserves clean, white sails, well shaped, so take care to cut them correctly.

5 If trying to fit deck features into the small space between the bulwarks is continuing to frustrate you, you might consider making your next schooner to a bigger scale, if you can find a suitable bottle. The scale card can be used to scale original illustrations up as well as down. A bigger model like this offers the opportunity to decorate the hull in good detail. The top of the freeboard, as shown in the illustration, can be a lighter colour than the lower hull, which might be black or another dark colour. A strand of gold cotton can be glued to the hull to separate the two colours, and a third band of red anti-fouling paint can be hinted at around the waterline, rising to follow the sheer at the bow.

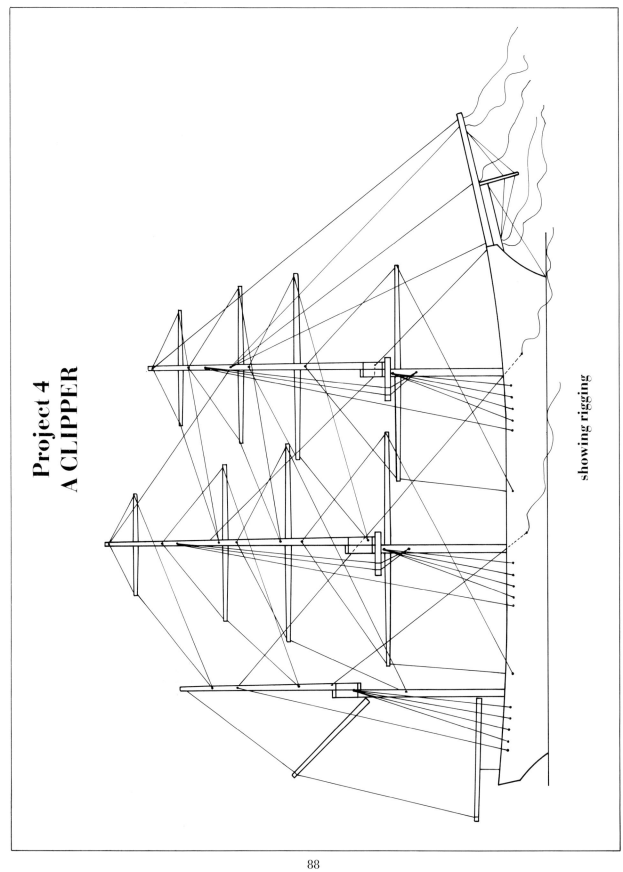

Project 4
A CLIPPER

showing rigging

The romance of the sailing ship is most often symbolized by a nineteenth century clipper ship in full sail, speeding from China round the Cape of Good Hope and back to England with a precious cargo of tea. These were fast, fine ships. Typically three masted, sharp bowed, sometimes sporting exaggerated sheers, they were built for speed – literally to 'clip' days off the east west passage and thus make fortunes for their owners. In the slang of the day, clipper came to mean anything first rate of its kind; the usage is lost now, but the legend of the great clippers lives on. They could sail home from Sydney in 70 days, making 20 knots, much faster than competing steamships: but their days of triumph were cut short when the Suez Canal opened up a much shorter route, and the steamships took over. The most famous of the clippers was the *Cutty Sark*, built on the Clyde of wood and iron in 1869 and now remarkably preserved in dry dock at Greenwich. A model clipper, all sails set, in a bottle, is quite a challenge, so if you have the chance to examine the real thing before you start, do take it. Look for details that you can add to your model, such as the decorations around the hull, the helmsmans's wheel, the figurehead (a new challenge!), but especially look at that wonderful rigging. It's no longer the original, of course, but it is

the closest you are ever likely to get to understanding the strength and power of a great sailing ship. But if the *Cutty Sark* isn't to hand, the rigging diagram above is a good place to start your model. Because this is a complicated ship to model (and probably it was a complicated ship to sail, too), there is a second drawing, of the sail plan, on page 90. Combining the two would have produced a result too confusing to follow, and when drawing up your own plans for a ship of this complexity from your own resources, separate rigging and sail plans are a great help.

The modelling process is well established by now, but there are a number of special considerations:

1 The hull should be made as large as practical. Try to track down a 'cider bottle', a generously sized bottle somewhat globular in shape, with a handle on one side and a bigger than usual neck. This will let you slide a hefty 'sausage' into the bottle, including a wider beamed hull and, if you are especially ambitious, a full set of stunsails. You might consider, now you are working on a bigger model, the alternative method of carving out the hull. The first cuts are made to produce the sheer, the curvature of the deck from stem to stern. Next, the deck is

exposed by carving away and down from the inside line of the bulwarks and finally, the job which is usually tackled first, the plan of the hull is carved from the block, outside and back to the bulwarks you have already shaped (see page 45).

2 The masts and spars are made in the conventional way, but with three double section masts and a greater number of yards than you have managed before, it becomes ever more important to keep all your pieces in an orderly manner so that they – and you – do not become confused. A well planned drilling chart is vital, not only because of the importance of completing all the drilling before you begin the rigging (a missing hole in a complicated model like this can be absolutely ruinous!), but also because if your plan shows that two closely placed holes are likely to interfere with each other, you have time to make the small design change necessary to correct this. Note also that two of the three masts in this model are fitted with tops, which are used to spread the shrouds, and that the bowsprit shrouds should be spread by two small spars (see figure 22, page 57).

3 With masts and spars completed, the rigging is relatively simple, but there

(continued on next page)

Project 4
A CLIPPER

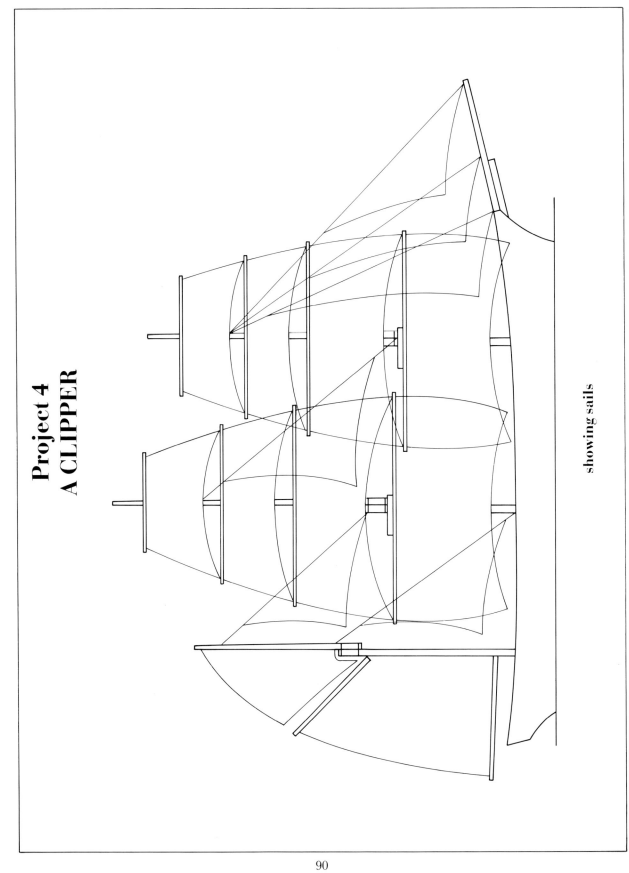

showing sails

(continued from previous page)

happens to be a lot of it. Take your time over it, and the detail and symmetry of it will give you years of pleasure, once the ship is in its bottle.

4 The same applies to the sails, the manufacture of which hardly varies from one model to another, but here – to stretch a point – you have a special responsibility. The *Cutty Sark* is the only surviving complete clipper, but she can never again set full sail; you can recreate a lost spectacle of maritime glory with your model.

A bigger hull and wider beam make for more deck fittings. You should find room for two or three deckhouses, three hatches, two companionways, and any other details your researches can find. There are typically three lifeboats on a clipper, two carried right way up on davits above the main deckhouse, aft of the mainmast, and one upside down on top of the forward deckhouse, aft of the forward mast. Making all of this requires ingenuity rather than technical expertise, and can be great fun once you have mastered the problems of scale involved.

Your model will look good with the hull painted in two colours. Use strands of coloured cotton to simulate coloured hull lines, and terminate them in a decorated scroll near the bow. Add similar decoration around the counter stern, and as a final touch put tiny, but evenly sized, blobs of white paint near the bottom of each shroud to represent a tightening block.

91

Project 5
S.S. *GREAT BRITAIN*

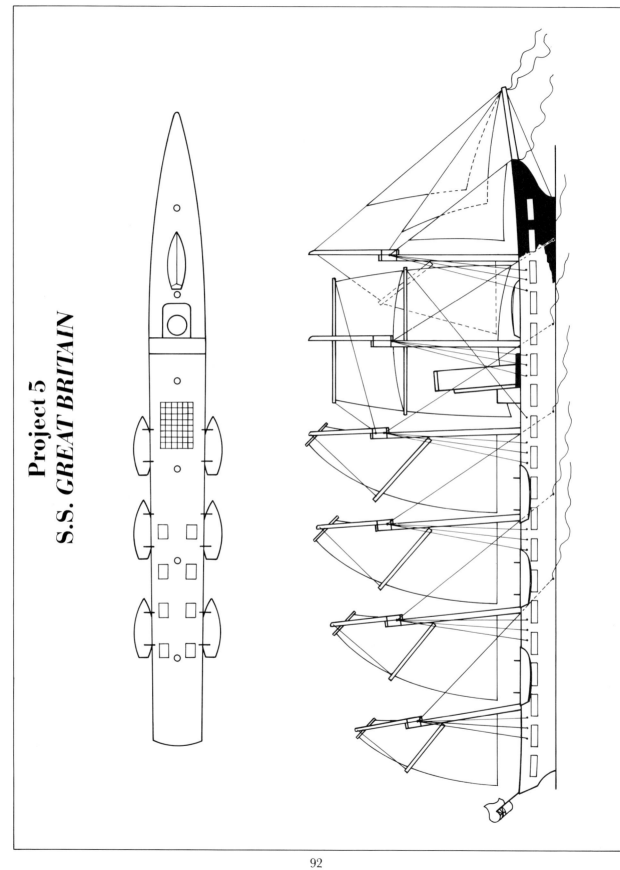

This unique hybrid steam sailing ship was built in Bristol in 1843 to the design of the great engineer Isambard Kingdom Brunel. She dates from that period in our maritime history when steam was seen first as a support for sail power and then as an alternative. Built of iron, she was a substantial vessel, 322 ft long, 51 ft in the beam, and would have been a paddle steamer but for a late change of mind on Brunel's part. (The S.S. *Great Eastern*, which followed in 1858, had a four-bladed propellor, sails *and* paddles.) When launched, she was the largest vessel in the world, but she was to be obsolete well before the end of the century. Never an especially beautiful ship, she carried progressively six, then five and finally just three masts, but our design is as she was originally. After various mis-adventures she ended up as a coal hulk in the Falklands, from where she was eventually rescued and towed back to Bristol, where she has been undergoing extensive renewal ever since. She makes an exciting model for display in a bottle, and will give you the chance to try out a few new ideas.

1 Like our previous model, this one will benefit from a big hull in a big bottle; it might well be the length of the ship which dictates its scale, bearing in mind that you don't want the stern jammed against the bottom of the bottle or the bowsprit out of the neck. This is the first hull we have considered with flush decks, without bulwarks. This makes it a great deal easier to carve, although you have to drill those diagonal holes for the shroud weaving, as shown in figure 29, page 64.

2 The spars and masts are simple enough, with each mast in two sections, joined without tops. One novelty is that the topsails terminate in their own small spar, which I can only call a top yard. Rather less obvious, but important to the overall appearance of the model, is the rake of the masts.

The aftermast leans noticeably sternwards, but the angle of rake of each mast reduces as the masts get closer to the bow, with the foremast vertical. This effect lends character to a strange ship, and is worth exaggerating slightly to add interest.

3 Rigging is straightforward, but time consuming: six masts, six sets of shrouds, six stays.

4 The sails are similarly straightforward. You might experiment with some sails furled, especially if you can find a contemporary illustration of the ship under part sail only.

5 A plan view has been added to the side elevation of this model, showing the eight small cabin tops and the large skylight above the main saloon, which can be made from a square of thin plastic, criss crossed with black lines. There is an upturned ship's boat on the foredeck, which will be much improved with a thin strip of silver foil along the keel. Six more ship's boats hang from davits over the ship's sides, and these have to be glued into position once the ship has been settled in the bottle. A loading stick charged with Blu-Tack will hold the boats firmly against the ship while the glue sets. The most obvious feature is the tall smoke stack assembly, raked rather more than the adjacent masts, standing immediately in front of an open bridge that stretches right across the deck. All this will require some skill to manoeuvre into position without damaging or tangling the rigging.

The hull should be black, with a white band running from stem to stern, broken at regular intervals by the black squares of the windows. This band can be vastly improved if a line of white cotton is glued along the top and bottom, to make the windows independent of the rest of the hull.

Glossary

athwart (athwartship) From side to side; across the ship, at right angles to the fore-and-aft centre line.

barquentine a three-masted vessel, with the fore-mast square-rigged, and the main-mast and mizen-mast fore-and-aft-rigged.

Bermuda (sail or rig) A three-cornered mainsail, or a ship which carries such a sail.

block An arrangement of grooved pulleys contained in a usually wooden block, used to gain a mechanical advantage, or to lead a rope in the required direction.

bobstay A wire or rope running from the end of the bowsprit to a point near the waterline on the bow and countering the upward pull of the sails that lead from the bowsprit.

boom A spar (round timber or metal pole) running along the foot of a sail.

bow The stem, or foremost part of a ship's hull.

bowsprit A spar projecting beyond the bow of the ship to which the head-sails are attached.

braces The ropes which run from the ends of the yards, which are the spars along the tops of square sails. They control the angle of the sails, which needs to be adjusted to suit the wind direction.

bulwarks The sides of a ship extending above the top deck, which prevent things or people from rolling off the deck into the sea.

clew The lower rear corner of a fore-and-aft sail, or both bottom corners of a square sail.

clipper A well designed, fine-lined, sharp-bowed sailing ship of high performance.

course Where this word does not mean 'direction', it refers to the lowest and usually the largest square sail on any of the masts; hence the main course is on the main mast.

crosstrees Stout cross-timbers running out from the sides of tall masts. Wires or ropes run from the mast head over the ends of the crosstrees and down to the deck, where they are secured. This helps to counter the tendency for the mast to bend sideways.

davits Constructions from which small boats are suspended and from which they can be swung out from the mother ship to be lowered to the water.

dolphin-striker A spar pointing downwards from the centre of the bowsprit, which with its associated wires works with the bobstay to stiffen the bowsprit.

foremast The mast nearest to the bow.

foresail There are many types of foresail, but it is a word loosely used to indicate any forward sail.

freeboard The height of a vessel between the water-line and the deck.

futtock plate A metal plate which is part of the topmast rigging in a large sailing ship.

gaff The spar which lies along the head of a four-sided fore-and-aft sail.

galleon A large vessel in use from the fifteenth to the seventeenth century with three or four decks and a stern high in relation to its comparatively short length.

gunwale The upper edge of a ship's side next to the bulwarks; a strengthening piece round the top edge of the hull.

headsail Any sail which is set before the fore-mast.

jack-staff The staff, or flagpole, at the forward end of a ship from which the Union Jack is flown. Note that the British national flag is the Union flag; it is only called the Union Jack when it is flown from a jack-staff on board a naval ship.

jib-boom A spar run out from the end of the bowsprit, used to set the jib sail.

leech The after edge of a sail.

luff The forward edge of a sail, running up the mast in the case of the mainsail.

marline spike A pointed metal tool for separating the strands of a rope when splicing.

mizen (or mizzen) The fore-and-aft sail hoisted on the mizen mast, which is the rearmost mast on a vessel with more than one mast.

port The left-hand side of a vessel, looking forward.

quarter The side of a vessel towards the stern.

royal A prefix meaning 'upper', but particularly applied to the topmost light-weather square sail.

scantlings Timbers shaped to their functional dimensions.

schooner A vessel with two or more masts and with fore-and-aft rigging (the foremast being the smaller).

sheer The fore-and-aft upward curve of a ship's deck.

sheet A rope fixed to the clew of a sail to control its set.

shrouds Wires which run from the mast to the edge of the deck to give the mast stability. They are secured to the deck by shroud plates.

spars The various lengths of timber or metal which are fitted to, or closely associated with, the sails.

square sail A sail which is roughly square in shape and is supported by a spar, or yard, to which the top edge is secured. The remainder of the sail is controlled by ropes, or sheets, from its bottom corners.

starboard The right-hand side of a vessel, looking forward.

staysail A triangular headsail which is hanked to a stay – a wire which, together with the shrouds, supports the mast and runs forward to the bowsprit or some other mid-ships (i.e. fore-and-aft) position.

stern The after end of a vessel.

stem The forward edge of the bow of a vessel; the foremost piece of the ship's frame, to which the sides are joined.

stunsail A narrow sail used to extend the area of a square sail and set from its outer edge, for use in light airs.

topgallant The lower topgallant is the fourth sail up on a mast carrying square sails. The upper topgallant is the fifth.

topsail The lower topsail is the second up and the upper topsail the third up on a square rigger. Otherwise it is a sail above a fore-and-aft main.

topmast When a mast is too long to be made from one length of timber it is extended with a topmast.

Turk's-head A woven design of rope or string to decorate a length of round wood, the end of a tiller – or even the neck of a bottle.

Union Jack The Union flag when flown from a jack-staff.

yard The spar which carries the top of a square sail and is at right angles to the mast which supports it.

Index

Page numbers in italics refer to illustrations.